MW01490790

QUICK & EASY

Carnivore Diet Cookbook for Seniors

Cooking Guide with Gut-Friendly, High-Protein, Low-carb Recipes for over 50 to improve hormone balance, inflammation, and boost Your Energy

By

Edward M. Corwin

Contents

Introduction

As we age, nutrition plays a crucial role in maintaining energy, mobility, and overall well-being. Yet, many diets feel overwhelming or fail to address the unique needs of seniors. The **carnivore diet** offers a simple, nourishing approach—focusing on high-quality animal-based foods that support joint health, digestion, and vitality.

This cookbook is designed **specifically for seniors**, making it easy to enjoy satisfying, nutrient-rich meals without complicated recipes or hard-to-find ingredients. Inside, you'll find:

- **Easy, senior-friendly recipes** with simple instructions.
- **Nutritional guidance** on the benefits of a carnivore lifestyle.
- **Practical tips** for meal planning, grocery shopping, and dining out.

Eating well shouldn't be a challenge. Whether you're new to the carnivore diet or looking for fresh ideas, this book will help you enjoy a healthier, more vibrant life—one delicious meal at a time.

Chapter 1: Understanding the Carnivore Diet

1- Benefits for Seniors

The **carnivore diet** offers a range of benefits specifically suited for seniors, addressing key concerns like muscle loss, joint health, digestion, and energy levels. As aging naturally leads to **muscle deterioration**, consuming high-quality **animal proteins** helps maintain **strength, mobility, and independence**. The **rich amino acid profile** of meats supports **muscle repair** and prevents frailty, reducing the risk of falls and injuries.

Inflammation is another major concern for seniors, often linked to **joint pain, arthritis, and metabolic conditions**. The carnivore diet, free from processed foods, sugars, and inflammatory grains, can **reduce chronic inflammation**, leading to **improved joint function and pain relief**. Additionally, its **high-fat content**, particularly from sources like **grass-fed meats and bone broths**, provides essential nutrients for **brain health**, helping to support memory, focus, and cognitive function.

Digestive issues such as bloating, acid reflux, and food intolerances become more common with age. By eliminating fiber-heavy or difficult-to-digest foods, the carnivore diet promotes gut health and nutrient absorption, leading to fewer digestive discomforts. The simplicity of this diet also makes meal planning easier, reducing the need for complex meal prep or calorie counting.

With benefits ranging from enhanced muscle retention and cognitive support to reduced inflammation and better digestion, the carnivore diet provides seniors with a sustainable, nutrient-dense approach to aging well, allowing them to maintain strength, energy, and overall well-being with ease.

A) Joint Pain Relief and Anti-Inflammatory Effects

Chronic joint pain and inflammation are common concerns for seniors, often caused by arthritis, aging, or dietary triggers. The carnivore diet can help **reduce inflammation naturally** by eliminating foods that contribute to joint discomfort, such as processed sugars, grains, and seed oils.

Animal-based foods provide **essential nutrients** that support joint health, including:
- **Collagen and Gelatin** – Found in bone broth and fatty cuts of meat, these compounds help maintain cartilage and reduce stiffness.
- **Omega-3 Fatty Acids** – Present in fatty fish and grass-fed meats, omega-3s help lower inflammation and ease joint pain.
- **Vitamin D and Calcium** – Essential for strong bones and reducing the risk of osteoporosis.

By focusing on high-quality proteins and healthy fats, the carnivore diet helps stabilize the body's inflammatory response, leading to noticeable relief in joint pain and stiffness. Many seniors experience improved mobility and reduced reliance on pain medications after transitioning to this way of eating. With fewer inflammatory foods in the diet and an increase in nutrient-dense meals, seniors can enjoy greater comfort, flexibility, and an active lifestyle well into their golden years.

B) Hormonal Balance and Bone Density Support

As we age, hormonal changes can affect **energy levels, metabolism, and bone health**. The carnivore diet helps **stabilize hormones naturally** by providing essential nutrients that support the body's regulatory functions.

- **Protein & Healthy Fats** – Animal-based foods supply cholesterol and amino acids, the building blocks for hormone production, helping maintain balanced energy and mood.
- **Vitamin D & Calcium** – Found in fatty fish, eggs, and dairy, these nutrients **strengthen bones** and reduce the risk of osteoporosis.
- **Collagen & Gelatin** – Support **bone structure and joint flexibility**, reducing the risk of fractures.
- **B Vitamins & Iron** – Aid in **red blood cell production** and improve circulation, keeping the body energized and resilient.

By eliminating **hormone-disrupting foods** like processed sugars and inflammatory seed oils, the carnivore diet promotes **stable blood sugar, improved bone density, and overall vitality**. Seniors following this approach often experience **better strength, fewer fractures, and greater hormonal balance**, leading to a healthier, more active lifestyle.

C) Energy Boosts and Fatigue Reduction

Fatigue and low stamina can make daily activities challenging, especially for seniors. The carnivore diet provides a **steady source of energy** by eliminating processed foods that cause blood sugar crashes and focusing on nutrient-dense animal products.

- **Stable Blood Sugar Levels** – Without refined carbs and sugars, the body maintains consistent energy throughout the day.
- **Protein-Powered Stamina** – High-quality proteins from meat support muscle function and prevent weakness.
- **Healthy Fats for Endurance** – Fats from animal sources provide long-lasting fuel, reducing feelings of exhaustion.
- **B Vitamins & Iron** – Found in red meat and organ meats, these nutrients improve oxygen flow, reducing fatigue and enhancing mental clarity.

By nourishing the body with **essential proteins, fats, and vitamins**, the carnivore diet helps seniors feel **more energetic, alert, and capable** in their daily lives. Many report waking up refreshed, experiencing fewer afternoon slumps, and maintaining stamina for physical activities and social engagements.

D) Enhanced Digestion for a Senior's Gastrointestinal System

Digestive issues become more common with age, often due to **food intolerances, slow metabolism, and gut inflammation**. The carnivore diet simplifies digestion by focusing on **easily absorbable animal-based foods** while eliminating common irritants like grains, legumes, and processed sugars.

- **Less Bloating & Gas** – Removing fiber-heavy and hard-to-digest plant foods reduces bloating and discomfort.
- **Gut-Healing Nutrients** – Bone broth, fatty meats, and organ meats provide **collagen, gelatin, and essential amino acids** that support gut lining repair.
- **Reduced Acid Reflux & Indigestion** – Without processed carbs and inflammatory foods, the digestive system functions more smoothly.
- **Improved Nutrient Absorption** – Animal-based foods are **rich in bioavailable vitamins and minerals**, making it easier for the body to absorb essential nutrients.

By **reducing digestive stress and promoting gut health**, the carnivore diet helps seniors **experience fewer stomach issues, improved regularity, and better overall digestion**, leading to greater comfort and well-being.

2- The Science of Easier Digestion as We Age

As we age, digestion slows down due to **reduced stomach acid production, weaker digestive enzymes, and changes in gut bacteria**. This makes it harder to break down and absorb nutrients from complex foods, often leading to bloating, discomfort, and nutrient deficiencies. The carnivore diet supports **easier digestion** by focusing on **simple, highly bioavailable** animal-based foods.

- **Efficient Nutrient Absorption** – Animal proteins and fats require **less digestive effort** compared to fiber-heavy plant foods.
- **Reduced Gut Irritation** – Eliminating grains, legumes, and processed sugars helps prevent **bloating, acid reflux, and inflammation.**
- **Collagen & Gelatin Support** – Found in meat and bone broth, these nutrients **strengthen the gut lining**, improving digestion and overall gut health.
- **No Anti-Nutrients** – Unlike plant-based foods, animal products **lack lectins, oxalates, and phytates**, which can interfere with mineral absorption.

By simplifying digestion, the carnivore diet allows seniors to **get more nourishment from their food with less digestive discomfort**, promoting overall health and vitality.

A) The Role of Collagen and Gelatin in Joint and Intestinal Health

Collagen and gelatin play a **vital role** in maintaining **joint flexibility and gut health**, both of which become increasingly important as we age. These proteins are naturally found in **bone broth, connective tissues, and fatty cuts of meat**, making them a key part of the carnivore diet.

Joint Health Benefits
- **Stronger Cartilage** – Collagen provides the **building blocks** for cartilage, helping to cushion joints and reduce stiffness.
- **Reduced Inflammation** – Gelatin contains **anti-inflammatory amino acids** like glycine, which help alleviate joint pain.
- **Improved Mobility** – Regular collagen intake supports **joint flexibility and strength**, making daily movements easier.

Intestinal Health Benefits
- **Gut Lining Repair** – Collagen and gelatin help **seal and strengthen the intestinal lining**, reducing issues like bloating and acid reflux.
- **Better Digestion** – Gelatin supports the production of stomach acid and digestive enzymes, promoting smoother digestion.
- **Reduced Inflammation** – Glycine and proline, found in gelatin, help calm **gut irritation and inflammation.**

By incorporating **collagen-rich foods**, seniors can experience **stronger joints, improved digestion, and overall better gut function**, leading to greater comfort and mobility.

B) Digestion-Friendly Meat Cuts and Preparation Methods

For seniors, choosing the **right meat cuts and cooking methods** can make digestion easier and meals more enjoyable. The carnivore diet emphasizes **tender, nutrient-rich cuts** that are easy to chew and digest while maximizing nutrient absorption.

Best Meat Cuts for Easy Digestion

- **Fatty Cuts** – Ribeye, short ribs, and lamb shoulder provide **healthy fats** that aid digestion and energy balance.
- **Ground Meats** – Ground beef, turkey, and lamb are **softer and easier to digest** than tougher cuts.
- **Bone Broth & Organ Meats** – Rich in **collagen and gelatin**, these support gut health and nutrient absorption.
- **Slow-Cooked Meats** – Braised beef, pot roast, and pulled pork **break down tough fibers**, making them gentle on digestion.

Best Preparation Methods

- **Slow Cooking & Braising** – Helps tenderize meat, making it easier to chew and digest.
- **Broiling & Roasting** – Enhances flavor without the need for heavy seasonings or oils.
- **Blending & Pureeing** – Useful for those with chewing difficulties, making meat easier to consume.

By selecting **easier-to-digest cuts** and **gentle cooking methods,** seniors can enjoy the benefits of the carnivore diet **without digestive discomfort,** ensuring meals are both nourishing and satisfying.

Chapter 2: Transitioning to the Carnivore Diet Safely

1- Starting the Carnivore Diet without side effects

Transitioning to the carnivore diet can bring significant health benefits, but a **gradual approach** helps minimize discomfort. Seniors may experience temporary changes as their body adapts, but with the right strategies, these effects can be reduced or avoided.

A) Identifying and overcoming initial symptoms like keto flu

When transitioning to the carnivore diet, some seniors may experience **temporary side effects** known as the **keto flu**. This happens as the body shifts from burning carbohydrates to using fats for energy. Symptoms can include **fatigue, headaches, muscle cramps, dizziness, and brain fog**, but they are manageable with the right approach.

How to Minimize Keto Flu Symptoms
- **Stay Hydrated** – Drink plenty of water and **increase electrolytes** (sodium, potassium, magnesium) to prevent dehydration.
- **Eat Enough Fat** – Healthy animal fats provide sustained energy and help the body adjust to fat-burning.
- **Get Enough Salt** – Adding salt to meals helps prevent weakness, headaches, and muscle cramps.
- **Take It Slow** – Gradually reducing carbs instead of cutting them overnight can ease the transition.
- **Prioritize Rest** – The body needs time to adjust, so **ensure adequate sleep and avoid overexertion.**

These symptoms **typically last a few days to a week** before energy levels stabilize. By **supporting the body with proper nutrition and hydration**, seniors can transition **smoothly and comfortably** into the carnivore lifestyle.

B) Optimal protein and fat intake for seniors

Balancing **protein and fat intake** is key to making the carnivore diet sustainable and beneficial for seniors. Proper macronutrient ratios support **muscle strength, energy levels, and overall health** while preventing nutrient deficiencies.

Protein Needs for Seniors
- Seniors need **adequate protein** to maintain **muscle mass, bone strength, and metabolic health.**
- Aim for **0.6 to 1 gram of protein per pound of ideal body weight** daily, depending on activity level.
- **Best protein sources**: Fatty cuts of beef, lamb, poultry, fish, eggs, and organ meats.

Importance of Healthy Fats
- Fats provide **steady energy, support brain health, and improve hormone regulation.**
- Seniors should get at least **60-70% of daily calories from fats** for optimal energy and digestion.
- **Best fat sources:** Ribeye, salmon, butter, tallow, ghee, egg yolks, and bone marrow.

Maintaining **the right balance** of protein and fat helps seniors feel **satisfied, energized, and nutritionally supported** while following the carnivore diet. Adjusting intake based on **hunger, activity level, and overall well-being** ensures long-term success.

2- How to prevent nutritional deficiencies

The carnivore diet provides **highly bioavailable nutrients**, but ensuring a well-rounded intake is essential for long-term health. Seniors need to focus on **variety and balance** to avoid potential deficiencies.

Key Nutrients to Prioritize
- **Vitamin B12 & Iron** – Essential for energy and brain health. Found in **red meat, liver, and eggs.**
- **Omega-3 Fatty Acids** – Support heart and brain function. Best sources include **fatty fish (salmon, sardines) and grass-fed meats.**
- **Vitamin D & Calcium** – Strengthen bones and prevent fractures. Get from **fatty fish, egg yolks, and dairy (if tolerated).**
- **Magnesium & Potassium** – Prevent muscle cramps and support hydration. Found in **meat, bone broth, and seafood.**
- **Collagen & Gelatin** – Improve joint and gut health. Obtain from **bone broth, skin-on meats, and connective tissue cuts.**

Tips for Avoiding Deficiencies
- Eat a **variety of meats**, including **organ meats** for maximum nutrients.
- Incorporate **bone broth** for minerals and gut health.
- Consider **electrolyte supplementation** if needed, especially in the early stages.

By **prioritizing nutrient-dense foods**, seniors can maintain **optimal health, energy, and longevity** while thriving on the carnivore diet.

3- Managing Electrolyte Balance with a Meat-Based Diet

Electrolytes play a crucial role in **hydration, muscle function, and overall well-being**. When transitioning to a carnivore diet, the body sheds excess water, which can lead to **electrolyte imbalances** if not properly managed. Seniors must ensure they are getting adequate levels of **sodium, potassium, and magnesium** to avoid fatigue, cramps, and dizziness.

Essential Electrolytes and Their Sources
- **Sodium** – Prevents dehydration and regulates blood pressure. Add **sea salt** to meals and drink **bone broth** daily.
- **Potassium** – Supports muscle function and heart health. Found in **meat, fish, and organ meats.**
- **Magnesium** – Helps with relaxation, sleep, and muscle recovery. Found in **seafood, bone broth, and mineral water.**

Tips for Maintaining Balance
- **Increase Salt Intake** – Add a pinch of salt to water or meals to prevent weakness and headaches.
- **Drink Bone Broth** – A natural source of essential minerals that supports digestion and hydration.
- **Stay Hydrated** – Drink plenty of **water, especially during the transition phase.**
- **Consider Electrolyte Supplements** – If experiencing persistent cramps or fatigue, a simple electrolyte supplement can help.

By **maintaining proper electrolyte levels**, seniors can **prevent common side effects**, stay hydrated, and feel energized while following the carnivore diet.

Chapter 3: Recipe Compendium

Section A: Anti-inflammatory and Easy-to-Digest Recipes

1- Bone Broths and Slow-Cooked Meats

Bone broths and slow-cooked meats are incredibly beneficial for seniors seeking anti-inflammatory support and easier digestion. Rich in collagen, gelatin, and amino acids, bone broth soothes the gut lining, supports joint health, and aids in repairing tissues. Slow-cooked meats become tender and easier to chew, while also releasing nutrients in a gentle, digestible form—perfect for those with sensitive stomachs or reduced appetite. These meals are warming, nourishing, and ideal for long-term gut and joint support.

Egg-based dishes and organ meats offer a powerhouse of nutrition with minimal ingredients. Eggs provide high-quality protein and healthy fats, while being soft, versatile, and easy to digest. Organ meats like liver, heart, and kidneys are loaded with vitamins A, B12, iron, and essential minerals that support energy, brain function, and hormone balance. Together, they deliver concentrated nutrients in a form the body can absorb efficiently, especially important for seniors looking to maintain strength and vitality through simple, nutrient-dense meals.

Classic Beef Bone Broth

 12-48 hours   8 cups

Ingredients:
- 3 lbs beef bones (knuckle bones, marrow bones, or oxtail)
- 12 cups water
- 2 tbsp apple cider vinegar
- 1 tsp sea salt
- 1 tsp black peppercorns
- 1 medium onion, quartered
- 2 carrots, chopped
- 2 celery stalks, chopped
- 4 cloves garlic, crushed
- 2 bay leaves

Instructions:
1. Roast bones at 400°F for 30 min to enhance flavor.
2. Soak bones in water + vinegar for 30 min.
3. Simmer, bringing to boil then reducing heat; skim foam.
4. Add veggies & seasoning.
5. Cook 12-48 hrs (The longer it simmers, the more nutrients are extracted).
6. Strain & store in jars (5 days fridge or freeze).

Calories per serving: 59 kcal
Protein: 8g | **Fat:** 2g | **Carbs:** 0g

Gut-Healing Chicken Bone Broth

 12-24 hours   8 cups

Ingredients:
- 3 lbs chicken bones
- 12 cups water
- 2 tbsp apple cider vinegar
- 1 tsp sea salt
- 1 tsp black peppercorns
- 1 onion, quartered
- 2 carrots, chopped
- 2 celery stalks, chopped
- 3 cloves garlic, crushed
- 2 bay leaves
- 1 tsp fresh thyme (optional)

Instructions:
1. Roast bones at 400°F for 30 min (optional for flavor).
2. Soak bones in water + vinegar for 30 min.
3. Simmer, bring to boil then reduce heat; skim foam.
4. Add veggies & seasoning.
5. Cook 12-24 hrs
6. Strain & store in jars (5 days fridge or freeze).

Calories per serving: 45 kcal
Protein: 9g | **Fat:** 1g | **Carbs:** 0g

Slow-Cooked Beef Short Ribs

🕐 6 hours   🍴 4

Ingredients:
- 3 lbs beef short ribs
- 4 cups beef broth
- 2 tbsp butter
- 1 onion, sliced
- 4 cloves garlic, minced
- 1 tsp sea salt
- 1 tsp black pepper
- 1 tsp thyme
- 1 bay leaf

Instructions:
1. Sear the ribs: Melt butter in a pan over medium-high heat. Brown ribs for 3-4 minutes per side.
2. Transfer to slow cooker: Place ribs, onion, garlic, and bay leaf into the slow cooker.
3. Add broth and seasonings: Pour in beef broth. Season with salt, pepper, and thyme.
4. Cook low and slow: Cover and cook on low for 6-8 hours until tender.
5. Serve warm

Calories per serving: 450 kcal
Protein: 40g | **Fat:** 30g | **Carbs:** 0g

Tender Braised Lamb Shanks

🕐 3 hours   🍴 4

Ingredients:
- 4 lamb shanks
- 4 cups beef broth
- 1 onion, chopped
- 4 cloves garlic, minced
- 2 tbsp butter
- 1 tsp sea salt
- 1 tsp black pepper
- 1 tsp rosemary
- 2 carrots, chopped
- 2 celery stalks, chopped

Instructions:
1. Preheat oven: Set to 325°F (163°C).
2. Brown the shanks: Heat butter in an oven-safe pot. Sear shanks for 4 minutes per side.
3. Add vegetables and seasoning: Stir in onion, garlic, carrots, celery, rosemary, salt, and pepper.
4. Braise in broth: Add beef broth, cover, and bake for 3 hours until fork-tender.
5. Serve warm

Calories per serving: 560 kcal
Protein: 48g | **Fat:** 38g | **Carbs:** 5g

Slow-Cooked Oxtail Stew

 4 hours   4

Ingredients:
- 3 lbs oxtail, cut into pieces
- 4 cups beef broth
- 1 onion, diced
- 4 cloves garlic, minced
- 2 tbsp butter
- 1 tsp sea salt
- 1 tsp black pepper
- 1 tsp thyme
- 2 carrots, chopped
- 2 bay leaves

Instructions:
1. Brown the oxtail: Heat butter in a large pot and sear oxtail for 5 minutes on each side.
2. Add broth and seasonings: Stir in onion, garlic, carrots, thyme, salt, and pepper. Pour in broth.
3. Simmer low and slow: Cover and let simmer for 4 hours until the meat is fall-apart tender.
4. Serve warm: Garnish with extra broth and enjoy.

Calories per serving: 550 kcal
Protein: 50g | **Fat:** 35g | **Carbs:** 0g

Simple Beef Pot Roast

 4-5 hours   6

Ingredients:
- 4 lbs beef roast
- 4 cups beef broth
- 1 onion, chopped
- 4 cloves garlic, minced
- 2 tbsp butter
- 1 tsp sea salt
- 1 tsp black pepper
- 2 carrots, chopped
- 2 celery stalks, chopped
- 1 tsp thyme

Instructions:
1. Sear the roast: Heat butter in a pot and sear the roast on all sides until browned.
2. Transfer to slow cooker: Place roast in a slow cooker and add onion, garlic, carrots, celery, salt, pepper, and thyme.
3. Add broth: Pour in beef broth and cover.
4. Slow cook: Cook on low for 4-5 hours until fork-tender.
5. Serve warm.

Calories per serving: 500 kcal
Protein: 55g | **Fat:** 30g | **Carbs:** 0g

Carnivore-Friendly Pork Shoulder

 6 hours   4

Ingredients:
- 3 lbs pork shoulder
- 2 tbsp beef tallow or butter
- 1 cup bone broth
- ½ tsp each: sea salt, black pepper (optional), garlic powder, smoked paprika, dried thyme
- ½ cup chopped onions (optional)
- ½ cup chopped zucchini or mushrooms (optional)

Instructions:
1. Pat pork dry; rub with salt, pepper, garlic powder, paprika, and thyme.
2. Heat tallow/butter in a skillet; sear pork 3-4 mins per side until golden.
3. Transfer to a slow cooker or oven-safe pot; add broth, onions, and zucchini/mushrooms.
4. Cover and cook on low for 6-8 hrs (or bake for 3-4 hrs) until fork-tender.
5. Shred pork, stir into juices, and serve hot with extra melted butter or tallow.

Calories per serving: 500 kcal
Protein: 55g | **Fat:** 30g | **Carbs:** 0g

Slow-Cooked Chicken Thighs

 6-8 hours   6

Ingredients:
- 6 bone-in, skin-on chicken thighs
- 2 tbsp butter or ghee
- 1 cup bone broth
- ½ tsp each: sea salt, black pepper (optional), garlic powder, rosemary or thyme
- ½ cup chopped onions or mushrooms (optional)

Instructions:
1. Pat chicken dry; rub with salt, pepper, garlic powder, and herbs.
2. Heat 1 tbsp butter in a skillet; sear thighs skin-side down for 3-4 mins.
3. Transfer to a slow cooker or oven dish; add broth and optional onions/mushrooms.
4. Cook on low for 6 hrs (or bake for 2.5-3 hrs) until tender.
5. Brush with remaining butter before serving.

Calories per serving: 380 kcal
Protein: 40g | **Fat:** 25g | **Carbs:** 0g

Easy Bone Marrow Broth

 12-24 hours   8

Ingredients:
- 2 lbs beef marrow bones (cut into sections)
- 8 cups water
- 1 tbsp apple cider vinegar
- ½ tsp sea salt (adjust to taste)
- ½ tsp black pepper (optional)
- ½ tsp dried thyme or rosemary

Instructions:
1. Rinse bones under cold water.
2. (Optional) Roast at 400°F (200°C) for 20 mins to enhance flavor.
3. Place bones in a pot or slow cooker. Add water, vinegar, salt, and optional spices.
4. Bring to a boil, then simmer on low for 12–24 hours.
5. Remove bones, strain broth through a fine sieve.
6. Store in glass jars. Keep refrigerated for 5 days or freeze for later.
7. Serve warm as a drink or use as a soup base.

Calories per serving: 500 kcal
Protein: 55g | **Fat:** 30g | **Carbs:** 0g

Beef Cheek Stew

 4-6 hours   8 4

Ingredients:
- 2 lbs beef cheeks (trimmed)
- 2 tbsp beef tallow or butter
- 4 cups bone broth
- ½ tsp sea salt (adjust to taste)
- ½ tsp black pepper (optional)
- ½ tsp garlic powder
- ½ tsp thyme or rosemary
- ½ cup diced onions or mushrooms (optional)

Instructions:
1. Pat beef cheeks dry and season with salt, pepper, garlic powder, and herbs.
2. Heat tallow or butter in a pot over medium-high. Sear beef cheeks 3–4 mins per side.
3. Add broth and optional veggies.
4. Cover and simmer on low for 4–6 hours (or 8 hours in a slow cooker) until fork-tender.
5. Shred meat and stir it back into the broth for added flavor.
6. Serve warm

Calories per serving: 500 kcal
Protein: 55g | **Fat:** 30g | **Carbs:** 0g

2- Egg-Based Dishes and Organ Meats for Optimal Nutrition

Classic Soft Scrambled Eggs

 5 Minutes   🍽 2

Ingredients:
- 4 large eggs
- 2 tbsp butter or ghee
- ¼ tsp sea salt

Instructions:
1. Whisk eggs with sea salt until smooth.
2. Melt butter in a non-stick pan over low heat.
3. Pour in eggs and stir gently with a spatula, scraping the bottom as they cook.
4. Continue stirring on low heat for 3-4 minutes until soft, creamy curds form.
5. Serve immediately for best texture.

Calories per serving: 200 kcal
Protein: 14g | **Fat:** 16g | **Carbs:** 1g

19

Nutrient-Dense Beef Liver and Onions

🕐 15 Minutes   🍽 2

Ingredients:
- ½ lb beef liver, thinly sliced
- 2 tbsp butter or ghee
- ½ cup onions, thinly sliced (optional)
- ½ tsp sea salt
- ½ tsp black pepper (optional)

Instructions:
1. Rinse and pat liver dry; soak in lemon water for 30 min if desired.
2. Heat 1 tbsp butter in a pan over medium heat.
3. Sauté onions for 3-4 min until soft.
4. Push onions aside, add remaining butter, and sear liver slices for 5 min per side.
5. Season with salt, pepper, stir with onions, and serve warm.

Calories per serving: 280 kcal
Protein: 30g | **Fat:** 12g | **Carbs:** 04g

Bacon and Egg Cups

 15 Minutes   2

Ingredients:
- 4 large eggs
- 4 strips of bacon
- ½ tsp sea salt (2g)
- ½ tsp black pepper (2g)
- ½ tsp garlic powder (2g)
- Smoked paprika (½ tsp): Adds a mild smokiness.
- Red pepper flakes (¼ tsp): For a little heat.
- Shredded cheese (¼ cup): For extra creaminess.

Instructions:
1. Preheat oven to 375°F (190°C).
2. Line a muffin tin with bacon strips, pressing them along the sides to form a cup.
3. Crack one egg into each bacon cup, then sprinkle with salt, black pepper, and garlic powder.
4. Bake for 12-15 minutes, or until the eggs are cooked to your preferred doneness.
5. Let cool for 2 minutes before removing from the tin, then serve warm.

Calories per serving: 410 kcal
Protein: 38g | **Fat:** 30g | **Carbs:** 01g

Carnivore Egg Custard

 30 Minutes 4

Ingredients:
- 4 large eggs (high in protein and healthy fats)
- 1 cup heavy cream
- 2 tbsp butter (for extra creaminess)
- ½ tsp sea salt (enhances flavor)
- ½ tsp vanilla extract (optional, for subtle sweetness)

Instructions:
1. Preheat oven to 325°F (160°C).
2. Grease 4 small ramekins with butter.
3. In a bowl, whisk eggs, heavy cream, salt, and vanilla extract until smooth.
4. Pour the mixture through a fine-mesh sieve to remove air bubbles.
5. Place ramekins in a baking dish and add hot water halfway up the sides.
6. Bake for 30-35 minutes, until the custard is set but slightly jiggly in the center.
7. Let cool for 10 minutes, then serve warm or refrigerate for a chilled custard.

Calories per serving: 180 kcal
Protein: 10g | **Fat:** 15g | **Carbs:** 01g

Fried Beef Kidney with Butter

 20-25 Minutes   2

Ingredients:
- 1 lb beef kidney (trimmed, cut into bite-sized pieces)
- 3 tbsp butter
- ½ tsp sea salt
- ½ tsp black pepper (optional)
- ½ tsp garlic powder (optional)

Instructions:
1. Rinse kidney under cold water; pat dry.
2. Trim membranes; cut into small pieces.
3. (Optional) Soak in lemon water or milk for 30 min to reduce strong flavor.
4. Heat 2 tbsp butter in a skillet over medium heat.
5. Add kidney pieces; sauté for 3-4 min, stirring occasionally.
6. Season with sea salt, black pepper, and garlic powder.
7. Stir in remaining 1 tbsp butter; cook 1-2 min until tender (avoid overcooking).
8. Serve hot with extra melted butter.

Calories per serving: 230 kcal
Protein: 25g | **Fat:** 12g | **Carbs:** 0g

Beef Heart Steak with Garlic Butter

 20 Minutes   2

Ingredients:
- 1 lb beef heart (trimmed, sliced into ½-inch steaks)
- 3 tbsp butter
- ½ tsp sea salt
- ½ tsp black pepper (optional)
- 1 garlic clove, minced
- 1 cup zucchini, sliced
- ½ cup mushrooms, sliced
- ½ tsp thyme or rosemary

Instructions:
1. Rinse beef heart; pat dry. Trim connective tissue and slice into steaks.
2. Season with sea salt and black pepper.
3. Heat 2 tbsp butter over medium-high; cook steaks 3-4 min per side.
4. Lower heat; add minced garlic and 1 tbsp butter. Spoon over steaks for 1 min.
5. Remove steaks; in same pan, sauté zucchini, mushrooms, and thyme 5-7 min.
6. Serve steaks with garlic butter and veggies on the side.

Calories per serving: 320 kcal
Protein: 40g | **Fat:** 18g | **Carbs:** 0g

Carnivore Omelet with Beef Liver

⏰ 15 Minutes 🍴 4

Ingredients:
- 3 large eggs
- ½ tsp sea salt
- ½ tsp black pepper (optional)
- 2 tbsp butter or ghee
- ½ cup beef liver, thinly sliced
- ½ cup spinach
- ¼ cup onions, diced
- ¼ cup mushrooms, sliced
- ½ tsp garlic powder
- ½ tsp smoked paprika
- ½ tsp dried oregano/thyme
- 1 tbsp hot sauce
- ½ tsp black pepper (optional)

Instructions:
1. Rinse, pat dry liver; slice thin. Heat 1 tbsp butter; sauté onions & mushrooms 3-4 min.
2. Add liver, spices; cook 20 min, flipping once.
3. Stir in spinach; cook 1 min.
4. Whisk eggs with salt & pepper.
5. Heat 1 tbsp butter; pour eggs into pan.
6. Cook 3-4 min, lift edges.
7. Add filling to one side; drizzle hot sauce if using. Fold omelet; cook 1 more min.

Calories per serving: 280 kcal
Protein: 30g | **Fat:** 18g | **Carbs:** 01g

Slow-Cooked Lamb Liver Pâté

⏰ 2 hours 🍴 6

Ingredients:
- ½ lb lamb liver, cut small
- 3 tbsp butter or ghee
- ¼ cup heavy cream
- ½ cup bone broth
- ½ tsp sea salt
- ½ tsp black pepper
- ½ tsp garlic powder
- ½ tsp smoked paprika
- ½ tsp dried thyme/rosemary
- 1 tbsp Worcestershire sauce/balsamic vinegar

Instructions:
1. Rinse, pat dry liver.
2. Sauté onions, celery, mushrooms in 1 tbsp butter for 4-5 min.
3. Add liver, garlic, paprika, thyme, Worcestershire; cook 3-4 min.
4. Transfer to pot/slow cooker; add broth + 1 tbsp butter.
5. Cover, simmer on low 1 hr, stir occasionally.
6. Cool slightly; blend with cream + 1 tbsp melted butter until smooth.
7. Pour into container; chill 2-3 hrs until firm.
8. Serve cold with meat or eggs.

Calories per serving: 250 kcal
Protein: 22g | **Fat:** 18g | **Carbs:** 1g

Duck Eggs Fried in Lard

 10 Minutes   2

Ingredients:
- 4 duck eggs
- 2 tbsp lard
- ½ tsp sea salt
- ¼ tsp black pepper
- ¼ tsp smoked paprika (optional)
- Garlic powder, chili flakes, or herb-infused lard (optional for flavor)

Instructions:
1. Melt lard in skillet over medium heat.
2. Crack eggs into skillet, keeping yolks intact.
3. Season with salt, pepper, and optional spices.
4. Cook 3-4 min for runny yolks; flip and cook 1-2 min for firmer yolks.
5. Plate eggs and drizzle with pan lard for extra richness.

Calories per serving: 420 kcal
Protein: 28g | **Fat:** 36g | **Carbs:** 1g

Rich Bone Marrow and Egg Scramble

 50 Minutes   3

Ingredients:
- 4 large eggs
- 2 tbsp heavy cream
- ½ tsp sea salt, black pepper
- ½ tsp garlic powder
- ½ tsp smoked paprika
- 6 beef marrow bones
- 1 tbsp Worcestershire sauce ½ tsp thyme or rosemary
- ½ cup diced onions
- ¼ cup sliced mushrooms
- ¼ cup chopped spinach
- 1 tbsp butter or ghee

Instructions:
1. Preheat oven to 400°F (200°C). Roast marrow bones 30 min. Scoop marrow; mix with thyme and Worcestershire (optional).
2. In skillet, melt butter. Sauté onions, mushrooms, spinach 3-4 min.
3. Whisk eggs, cream, salt, pepper, garlic powder, paprika.
4. Pour into skillet; stir gently 2-3 min until fluffy.
5. Fold in roasted marrow; garnish with extra marrow or butter.

Calories per serving: 320 kcal
Protein: 20g | **Fat:** 28g | **Carbs:** 01g

Section B: Collagen and Mineral-Rich Recipes

Stews and braises with cartilage

This section focuses on recipes that utilize cuts of meat rich in cartilage and connective tissue, which break down beautifully during slow cooking. These stews and braises are packed with collagen, a protein that supports joint flexibility, skin elasticity, and gut health—especially vital for seniors. As the cartilage softens during the cooking process, it releases valuable minerals like calcium, magnesium, and phosphorus, helping to support bone density and reduce inflammation. These comforting, slow-cooked meals are not only deeply flavorful but also easy to digest and nourishing for the aging body.

Omega-3 Rich Fish Dishes – For Inflammation Management

This section highlights fish-based recipes that are naturally high in omega-3 fatty acids, known for their powerful anti-inflammatory properties. These healthy fats help reduce stiffness, support brain health, and may ease symptoms related to conditions like arthritis or high blood pressure—common concerns among seniors. By including easy-to-make meals with salmon, mackerel, sardines, and other oily fish, this section offers both variety and therapeutic value. These dishes are light, heart-healthy, and ideal for anyone seeking to manage inflammation through nourishing, low-carb, animal-based meals.

1- Stews and braises with cartilage

Braised Beef Shank with Bone Broth

⏰ 3 hours   🍽 4

Ingredients:
- 2 lbs beef shank (bone-in)
- 1 tbsp beef tallow or butter
- 2 cups bone broth
- 1 cup diced onions
- ½ cup chopped carrots
- ½ tsp sea salt
- ½ tsp black pepper
- ½ tsp garlic powder
- ½ tsp dried thyme

Instructions:
1. Heat beef tallow in a pot over medium heat and sear the beef shank for 4 minutes per side until browned.
2. Add onions, carrots, and bone broth, then season with salt, pepper, garlic powder, and thyme.
3. Reduce heat to low, cover, and simmer for 3 hours.
4. Once the meat is tender and falling off the bone, serve hot with broth.

Calories per serving: 410 kcal
Protein: 48g | **Fat:** 22g | **Carbs:** 02g

Slow-Cooked Oxtail Stew

⏰ 4 hours   🍽 4

Ingredients:
- 2 lbs oxtail (cut into sections)
- 1 tbsp butter
- 2 cups bone broth
- 1 cup diced tomatoes
- ½ cup diced celery
- ½ cup diced carrots
- ½ tsp smoked paprika
- ½ tsp garlic powder
- ½ tsp dried oregano
- ½ tsp sea salt

Instructions:
1. Melt butter in a large pot over medium heat and brown oxtail on all sides for 5 minutes.
2. Add bone broth, tomatoes, celery, carrots, and seasonings. Stir well.
3. Cover and reduce to low heat, simmering for 4 hours, stirring occasionally.
4. Once the meat is tender and the broth is rich, serve warm.

Calories per serving: 480 kcal
Protein: 50g | **Fat:** 28g | **Carbs:** 2g

Lamb Neck Stew with Bone Broth

⏰ 3.5 hours   🍽4

Ingredients:
- 2 lbs lamb neck (bone-in, cut into sections)
- 2 tbsp butter or ghee
- 2 cups bone broth
- 1 cup diced onions
- ½ cup diced turnips (low-carb alternative to potatoes)
- ½ cup diced carrots
- ½ tsp dried rosemary
- ½ tsp sea salt
- ½ tsp black pepper
- ½ tsp garlic powder

Instructions:
1. Heat butter or ghee in a large pot over medium-high heat and sear the lamb neck pieces for 5 minutes, turning occasionally.
2. Add onions, turnips, carrots, and bone broth, then stir in rosemary, salt, pepper, and garlic powder.
3. Cover and simmer on low heat for 3.5 hours, stirring occasionally.
4. Once the meat is tender and falling off the bone, serve warm with broth.

Calories per serving: 460 kcal
Protein: 45g | **Fat:**30g | **Carbs:** 0g

Pork Hock and Cabbage Stew

⏰ 4 hours   🍽4

Ingredients:
- 2 lbs pork hock (bone-in)
- 2 tbsp beef tallow or butter
- 2 cups bone broth
- 1 cup shredded cabbage
- ½ cup diced onions
- ½ tsp smoked paprika
- ½ tsp garlic powder
- ½ tsp dried thyme
- ½ tsp sea salt

Instructions:
1. Melt tallow or butter in a large pot over medium heat, then sear pork hock on all sides for 5 minutes.
2. Add bone broth, cabbage, onions, and seasonings, then stir well.
3. Cover and reduce to low heat, simmering for 4 hours until the pork is fall-apart tender.
4. Shred the meat, stir into the broth, and serve hot.

Calories per serving: **49**0 kcal
Protein: 52g | **Fat:** 32g | **Carbs:** 0g

Beef Tendon and Mushroom Stew

 4 hours   4

Ingredients:
- 1.5 lbs beef tendon (cut into pieces)
- 2 tbsp butter or ghee
- 2 cups bone broth
- 1 cup sliced mushrooms
- ½ cup diced onions
- ½ tsp sea salt
- ½ tsp black pepper
- ½ tsp dried oregano

Instructions:
1. Melt butter or ghee in a pot over medium-high heat and lightly brown the beef tendon.
2. Add bone broth, mushrooms, onions, and seasonings, then stir.
3. Cover and simmer on low heat for 4 hours, stirring occasionally.
4. Once the tendons become soft and gelatinous, serve warm.

Calories per serving: 420 kcal
Protein: 42g | **Fat:** 28g | **Carbs:** 0g

Duck Stew with Cartilage

 4 hours   4

Ingredients:
- 1 whole duck (with skin and cartilage, cut into pieces) 2 tbsp duck fat or lard (30g)
- 4 cups bone broth (1 liter)
- 1 tsp sea salt (adjust to taste)
- ½ tsp black pepper
- Garlic powder.
- Smoked paprika.
- Fresh thyme or rosemary.
- Red pepper flakes

Instructions:
1. Heat fat in a large pot over medium-high.
2. Brown duck pieces 5-7 min.
3. Add broth, salt, pepper, and seasonings.
4. Simmer covered on low 1.5-2 hrs, stirring occasionally, until duck is tender and cartilage soft.
5. Ladle into bowls, drizzle with broth, and garnish with herbs.

Calories per serving: 680 kcal
Protein: 55g | **Fat:** 48g | **Carbs:** 0g

Slow-Cooked Beef Ribs in Bone Broth

 4.5 hours   🍽 4

Ingredients:
- 2 lbs beef short ribs
- 2 tbsp beef tallow or butter
- 2 cups bone broth
- 1 cup diced tomatoes
- ½ cup chopped carrots
- ½ tsp dried thyme
- ½ tsp sea salt
- ½ tsp black pepper

Instructions:
1. Melt tallow or butter in a pot over medium heat and sear the ribs for 5 minutes per side.
2. Add bone broth, tomatoes, carrots, and seasonings, then cover.
3. Simmer on low heat for 4.5 hours, stirring occasionally.
4. Once the ribs are tender and the broth is rich, serve hot.

Calories per serving: 520 kcal
Protein: 55g | **Fat:** 35g | **Carbs:** 0g

Goat Meat and Collagen Stew

 3.5 hours   🍽 4

Ingredients:
- 2 lbs goat meat (bone-in)
- 2 tbsp butter
- 2 cups bone broth
- ½ cup chopped turnips
- ½ cup diced onions
- ½ tsp garlic powder
- ½ tsp smoked paprika
- ½ tsp sea salt

Instructions:
1. Heat butter in a pot over medium-high heat and sear goat meat for 5 minutes.
2. Add bone broth, turnips, onions, and seasonings, then stir well.
3. Cover and simmer on low heat for 3.5 hours until the meat is tender.
4. Serve hot with broth.

Calories per serving: 440 kcal
Protein: 50g | **Fat:** 82g | **Carbs:** 0g

Duck Breast Stew

⏰ 1.5 hours 🍴 4

Ingredients:
- 2 duck breasts (500g)
- 2 tbsp duck fat or tallow (30g)
- 4 cups bone broth (1 liter)
- 1 tsp sea salt (5g)
- ½ tsp black pepper (2g)
- ½ tsp garlic powder (2g)
- ½ tsp smoked paprika (2g)
- ½ tsp dried thyme (2g)
- Red pepper flakes (¼ tsp)
- Bay leaf (1 leaf)
- Apple cider vinegar (1 tbsp)

Instructions:
1. Heat duck fat in a Dutch oven over medium-high heat. Sear duck breasts skin-side down for 4-5 min until golden; flip and cook 2 min more. Remove.
2. Deglaze pan with bone broth, scraping browned bits. Add all seasonings, bay leaf, and vinegar if using.
3. Return duck breasts, cover, and simmer on low 1.5 hrs, stirring occasionally. Once tender, discard bay leaf, slice duck, and serve in broth. Drizzle extra duck fat if desired.

Calories per serving: 650 kcal
Protein: 58g | **Fat:** 45g | **Carbs:** 0g

Duck Wing and Cartilage Stew

⏰ 3 hours 🍴 4

Ingredients:
- 1.5 lbs duck wings (bone-in)
- 2 tbsp duck fat or butter
- 2 cups bone broth
- ½ cup diced onions
- ½ cup chopped turnips
- ½ tsp dried oregano
- ½ tsp sea salt
- ½ tsp black pepper

Instructions:
1. Heat duck fat or butter in a pot over medium-high heat and sear duck wings for 4 minutes per side.
2. Add bone broth, onions, turnips, and seasonings, stirring well.
3. Cover and simmer on low heat for 3 hours, stirring occasionally.
4. Once the cartilage is soft and the broth is rich, serve warm.

Calories per serving: 450 kcal
Protein: 46g | **Fat:** 30g | **Carbs:** 0g

Omega-3 Rich Fish Dishes for Inflammation Management

Pan-Seared Salmon with Garlic Butter

 10 Minutes 2

Ingredients:
- 2 salmon fillets (6 oz each)
- 2 tbsp butter or ghee
- ½ tsp sea salt
- ½ tsp black pepper
- ½ tsp garlic powder
- ½ tsp smoked paprika
- 1 tbsp lemon juice

Instructions:
1. Heat butter or ghee in a pan over medium-high heat.
2. Season salmon fillets with sea salt, black pepper, garlic powder, and smoked paprika.
3. Place salmon skin-side down and sear for 4-5 minutes, then flip and cook for another 3 minutes.
4. Drizzle with lemon juice, remove from heat, and serve warm.

Calories per serving: 420 kcal
Protein: 40g | **Fat:** 28g

Baked Sardines with Olive Oil and Herbs

 20 Minutes 2

Ingredients:
- 4 fresh sardines (whole, cleaned)
- 2 tbsp olive oil
- ½ tsp sea salt
- ½ tsp dried thyme
- ½ tsp garlic powder
- 1 tbsp lemon juice

Instructions:
1. Preheat grill to medium-high; grease grates with butter or ghee.
2. Season fillets with salt, dill, and pepper.
3. Grill 5-6 min per side until cooked through, flipping once.
4. Drizzle with lemon juice and serve hot.

Calories per serving: 380 kcal
Protein: 42g | **Fat:** 25g

Grilled Mackerel with Lemon and Dill

Ingredients:
- 2 salmon fillets (6 oz each)
- 2 tbsp butter or ghee
- ½ tsp sea salt
- ½ tsp black pepper
- ½ tsp garlic powder
- ½ tsp smoked paprika
- 1 tbsp lemon juice

Instructions:
1. Heat butter or ghee in a pan over medium-high heat.
2. Season salmon fillets with sea salt, black pepper, garlic powder, and smoked paprika.
3. Place salmon skin-side down and sear for 4-5 minutes, then flip and cook for another 3 minutes.
4. Drizzle with lemon juice, remove from heat, and serve warm.

Calories per serving: 420 kcal
Protein: 40g | **Fat:** 28g

Baked Sardines with Olive Oil and Herbs

⏰ 20 Minutes   🍽 2

Ingredients:
- 4 fresh sardines (whole, cleaned)
- 2 tbsp olive oil
- ½ tsp sea salt
- ½ tsp dried thyme
- ½ tsp garlic powder
- 1 tbsp lemon juice

Instructions:
1. Preheat grill to medium-high; grease grates with butter or ghee.
2. Season fillets with salt, dill, and pepper.
3. Grill 5-6 min per side until cooked through, flipping once.
4. Drizzle with lemon juice and serve hot.

Calories per serving: 380 kcal
Protein: 42g | **Fat:** 25g

Grilled Mackerel with Lemon and Dill

⏰ 12 Minutes 🍽 2

Ingredients:
- 2 mackerel fillets (6 oz each)
- 1 tbsp butter or ghee
- ½ tsp sea salt
- ½ tsp dried dill
- ½ tsp black pepper
- 1 tbsp lemon juice

Instructions:
1. Heat a grill to medium-high heat and grease with butter or ghee.
2. Season mackerel fillets with salt, dill, and black pepper.
3. Grill for 5-6 minutes per side, flipping once.
4. Drizzle with lemon juice and serve immediately.

Calories per serving: 410 kcal
Protein: 38g | **Fat:** 28g

Butter-Poached Mahi-Mahi with Herbs

⏰ 10 Minutes 🍽 2

Ingredients:
- 2 mahi-mahi fillets (6 oz each)
- 3 tbsp butter
- ½ cup bone broth
- ½ tsp sea salt
- ½ tsp black pepper
- ½ tsp dried thyme
- 1 tbsp lemon juice

Instructions:
1. In a saucepan, melt butter over medium-low; add broth, salt, pepper, and thyme.
2. Bring to a light simmer.
3. Place fillets in broth, partially submerged.
4. Cover and poach on low for 12-15 min, flipping once, until opaque and flaky.
5. Drizzle with lemon juice; spoon butter broth over fillets before serving.

Calories per serving: 450 kcal
Protein: 44g | **Fat:** 30g

Pan-Fried Herring with Mustard Butter

 15 Minutes   2

Ingredients:

- 4 herring fillets (boneless)
- 2 tbsp butter (for frying and richness)
- ½ tsp sea salt (enhances natural flavor)
- ½ tsp black pepper (mild spice)
- 1 tbsp Dijon mustard (adds depth and tang)
- 1 tbsp lemon juice (for balance)

Instructions:

1. Pat herring fillets dry and season with sea salt and black pepper.
2. Heat butter in a skillet over medium heat.
3. Place fillets skin-side down and fry for 7 minutes per side until golden brown.
4. Remove from heat and brush with Dijon mustard and lemon juice before serving warm.

Calories per serving: 350 kcal
Protein: 42g | **Fat:** 24g

Tuna and Egg Salad with Olive Oil

 10 Minutes   2

Ingredients:

- 1 can tuna (in olive oil, drained)
- 3 hard-boiled eggs (chopped)
- 2 tbsp olive oil (for creaminess)
- ½ tsp sea salt (enhances taste)
- ½ tsp black pepper (for balance)1 can tuna (in olive oil, drained)
- 2 hard-boiled eggs (chopped)
- 2 tbsp olive oil (for creaminess)
- ½ tsp sea salt (enhances taste)
- ½ tsp black pepper (for balance)

Instructions:

1. In a bowl, mix tuna, chopped eggs, olive oil, salt, and pepper.
2. Stir well until combined and creamy.
3. Serve immediately.

Calories per serving: 380 kcal
Protein: 42g | **Fat:** 28g

Baked Trout with Lemon and Herbs

⏰ 20 Minutes   🍽 2

Ingredients:
- 2 trout fillets (6 oz each)
- 1 tbsp butter
- ½ tsp sea salt
- ½ tsp dried thyme
- 1 tbsp lemon juice

Instructions:
1. Preheat oven to 375°F (190°C).
2. Place trout fillets in a baking dish, season with salt, thyme, and lemon juice, then dot with butter.
3. Bake for 20 minutes until flaky.
4. Serve warm.

Calories per serving: 390 kcal
Protein: 44g | **Fat:** 26g

Sardine and Egg Scramble

⏰ 10 Minutes   🍽 2

Ingredients:
- 1 can sardines (in olive oil, drained)
- 4 large eggs
- 2 tbsp butter
- ½ tsp sea salt
- ½ tsp black pepper

Instructions:
1. Heat butter in a skillet over medium heat.
2. Whisk eggs with salt and pepper, then pour into the pan.
3. Add sardines, scrambling gently for 3-4 minutes.
4. Serve warm.

Calories per serving: 410 kcal
Protein: 44g | **Fat:** 28g

Seared Halibut with Garlic Butter

 5 Minutes   2

Ingredients:
- 2 halibut fillets (6 oz each)
- 2 tbsp butter
- ½ tsp sea salt
- ½ tsp garlic powder

Instructions:
1. Heat butter in a pan over medium-high heat.
2. Season halibut with salt and garlic powder, then sear for 5-6 minutes per side.
3. Serve warm with extra butter.

Crispy Salmon Skin Chips

15 Minutes   2

Ingredients:
- 2 salmon skins (cleaned and patted dry)
- 1 tbsp butter or ghee (for crisping)
- ½ tsp sea salt (enhances taste)
- ½ tsp black pepper (for mild spice)
- ½ tsp smoked paprika (optional, for depth)

Instructions:
1. Pat salmon skins dry and season with salt, pepper, and smoked paprika.
2. Heat butter or ghee in a skillet over medium-high heat.
3. Cook the skins for 4-5 minutes per side, pressing lightly to ensure crisping.
4. Let cool slightly and enjoy warm or as a crunchy snack

Calories per serving: 430 kcal
Protein: 42g | **Fat:** 28g

Calories per serving: 280 kcal
Protein: 30g | **Fat:** 18g

Section C: Energy Boosting and Hormone Supporting Recipes

Grass-fed beef and butter dishes

They offer a powerful combination of protein and healthy fats that help sustain energy throughout the day—especially important for seniors who want to stay active without sudden fatigue. Grass-fed beef is richer in omega-3s and conjugated linoleic acid (CLA), which may support hormone health and reduce inflammation. Paired with butter, which is a natural source of vitamin A and K2, these meals can also help maintain healthy cholesterol levels and support cognitive function.

Organ meats like liver and heart

They are nutritional powerhouses packed with essential vitamins that play a direct role in hormone production and energy metabolism. Liver is especially rich in B vitamins, iron, and vitamin A, all of which are vital for cellular energy and healthy immune response. Heart meat is an excellent source of CoQ10, a nutrient that supports heart health and mitochondrial energy production. These ingredients are ideal for seniors needing a nutrient-dense boost without relying on complex meal prep.

Grass-fed beef and butter dishes

Butter-Basted Grass-Fed Ribeye Steak

 20 Minutes 2

Ingredients:
- 2 grass-fed ribeye steaks (8 oz each)
- 3 tbsp butter
- ½ tsp sea salt
- ½ tsp black pepper
- 2 crushed garlic cloves
- ½ tsp dried rosemary (optional)

Instructions:
1. Pat steaks dry and season both sides with salt and pepper.
2. Heat 1 tbsp butter in a hot skillet. Sear steaks for 7 minutes per side until a crust forms.
3. Reduce to medium heat. Add remaining butter, garlic, and rosemary. Spoon melted butter over the steaks for 1-2 minutes.
4. Rest steaks for 5 minutes before slicing. Serve warm, drizzled with the infused butter.

Calories per serving: 650 kcal
Protein: 52g | **Fat:** 48g

Grass-Fed Beef Burgers with Butter Topping

 12 Minutes 2

Ingredients:
- 1 lb grass-fed ground beef
- 2 tbsp butter (for topping)
- ½ tsp sea salt (enhances taste)
- ½ tsp black pepper (mild spice)
- ½ tsp garlic powder (adds depth)

Instructions:
1. Combine beef with salt, pepper, and garlic powder. Form into two patties.
2. Grill or pan-cook over medium-high heat for 5-6 minutes per side.
3. Remove from heat and top each patty with 1 tbsp butter to melt.
4. Serve hot, optionally with scrambled eggs or sautéed mushrooms.

Calories per serving: 520 kcal
Protein: 45g | **Fat:** 38g

Slow-Cooked Grass-Fed Beef Short Ribs

 4 Hours   2

Ingredients:
- 2 lbs grass-fed beef short ribs
- 3 tbsp butter (adds richness)
- 2 cups bone broth (for moisture)
- ½ tsp sea salt (enhances taste)
- ½ tsp black pepper (for mild spice)
- ½ tsp smoked paprika
- ½ cup diced onions

Instructions:
1. Melt 1 tbsp butter in a pot over medium-high heat.
2. Sear ribs for 4-5 minutes per side until browned.
3. Add bone broth, onions, and seasonings, then cover and simmer on low heat for 4 hours.
4. Stir in remaining butter before serving for added richness.
5. Serve warm with extra cooking broth.

Calories per serving: 610 kcal
Protein: 42g | **Fat:** 48g

Garlic Butter Grass-Fed Beef Tenderloin

 15 Minutes   4

Ingredients:
- 2 grass-fed beef tenderloin steaks (6 oz each)
- 3 tbsp butter (for basting)
- ½ tsp sea salt (enhances natural flavor)
- ½ tsp black pepper (adds balance)
- 1 garlic clove, minced (for extra depth)

Instructions:
1. Pat tenderloin steaks dry and season with salt and black pepper.
2. Heat 1 tbsp butter in a skillet over high heat.
3. Sear steaks for 4-5 minutes per side.
4. Reduce heat to medium, add remaining butter and garlic, and baste for 2 minutes.
5. Let rest for 5 minutes, then serve warm.

Calories per serving: 610 kcal
Protein: 42g | **Fat:** 48g

Butter-Braised Grass-Fed Beef Brisket

 4.5 hours 🍴 4

Ingredients:
- 2.5 lbs grass-fed beef brisket
- 3 tbsp butter (for basting and moisture)
- 2 cups bone broth (adds depth and richness)
- ½ tsp sea salt (enhances taste)
- ½ tsp black pepper (for balance)
- ½ tsp garlic powder (adds depth)
- ½ tsp smoked paprika (optional, for warmth)

Instructions:
1. Melt 1 tbsp butter in a pot over medium-high heat.
2. Sear brisket for 5 minutes per side until golden brown.
3. Add bone broth, salt, black pepper, garlic powder, and paprika.
4. Cover and simmer on low heat for 4.5 hours, flipping occasionally.
5. In the last 30 minutes, stir in the remaining 2 tbsp butter for added richness.
6. Rest for 5 minutes, then slice and serve with broth.

Calories per serving: 600 kcal
Protein: 55g | **Fat:** 40g | **Carbs:** 0g

Butter-Fried Grass-Fed Beef Liver

🕑 25 Minutes 🍴 2

Ingredients:
- ½ lb grass-fed beef liver (thinly sliced)
- 3 tbsp butter (for frying and extra richness)
- ½ tsp sea salt (enhances taste)
- ½ tsp black pepper (for mild spice)
- 1 garlic clove, minced (optional, for extra depth)
- 1 tbsp lemon juice (balances flavor)

Instructions:
1. Rinse beef liver under cold water and pat dry.
2. (Optional) Soak in lemon water for 30 minutes to reduce the strong taste.
3. Melt 2 tbsp butter in a pan over medium heat.
4. Add liver slices and cook for 25 minutes, flipping once.
5. Stir in remaining butter, garlic, and lemon juice.
6. Sauté for another 30 seconds, then serve warm.

Calories per serving: 420 kcal
Protein: 50g | **Fat:** 28g | **Carbs:** 0g

Grass-Fed Beef Tallow Meatballs

 25 Minutes   4

Ingredients:
- 1 lb grass-fed ground beef
- 2 eggs
- 2 tbsp beef tallow
- ½ tsp sea salt
- ½ tsp black pepper
- ½ tsp garlic powder
- ½ tsp dried oregano

Instructions:
1. Preheat oven to 375°F (190°C).
2. In a bowl, combine ground beef, eggs, tallow, and seasonings. Mix gently until just combined.
3. Form golf ball-sized meatballs and arrange on a greased or parchment-lined baking sheet.
4. Bake for 20-25 minutes until browned and cooked through.
5. Optional: Broil for 2-3 mins or pan-sear briefly in tallow for a crispy crust.
6. Serve hot; great with a drizzle of extra tallow for richness.

Calories per serving: 480 kcal
Protein: 42g | **Fat:** 34g | **Carbs:** 0g

Butter-Braised Grass-Fed Beef Cheeks

 4 hours   4

Ingredients:
- 2 lbs grass-fed beef cheeks
- 3 tbsp butter (for basting)
- 2 cups bone broth (adds depth and moisture)
- ½ tsp sea salt (enhances taste)
- ½ tsp black pepper (for balance)
- ½ tsp smoked paprika (adds warmth)
- ½ cup diced onions (adds mild sweetness)

Instructions:
1. Melt 1 tbsp butter in a pot over medium-high heat.
2. Sear beef cheeks for 4-5 minutes per side.
3. Add bone broth, onions, and seasonings.
4. Cover and simmer on low heat for 4 hours, stirring occasionally.
5. Stir in remaining 2 tbsp butter before serving.
6. Serve warm with cooking broth.

Calories per serving: 580 kcal
Protein: 52g | **Fat:** 42g | **Carbs:** 0g

Butter-Seared Grass-Fed New York Strip Steak

 15 Minutes   2

Ingredients:
- 2 grass-fed New York strip steaks (8 oz each)
- 3 tbsp butter (for basting)
- ½ tsp sea salt (enhances taste)
- ½ tsp black pepper (for mild spice)
- ½ tsp dried rosemary (optional, for aroma)

Instructions:
1. Pat steaks dry and season with salt, black pepper, and rosemary.
2. Heat 1 tbsp butter in a skillet over medium-high heat.
3. Sear steaks for 3-4 minutes per side.
4. Reduce heat, add remaining butter, and spoon over the steaks for 2 minutes.
5. Let the steaks rest for 8 minutes, then serve warm.

Calories per serving: 620 kcal
Protein: 50g | **Fat:** 46g | **Carbs:** 0g

Slow-Cooked Buttered Grass-Fed Oxtail

 4 hours 4

Ingredients:
- 2 lbs grass-fed oxtail
- 3 tbsp butter (adds richness)
- 2 cups bone broth (for deep flavor)
- ½ tsp sea salt (enhances taste)
- ½ tsp black pepper (for balance)
- ½ cup diced onions (adds mild sweetness)
- ½ tsp dried thyme (optional, for aroma)

Instructions:
1. Heat 1 tbsp butter in a pot over medium-high heat.
2. Brown oxtail pieces for 5 minutes per side.
3. Add bone broth, onions, salt, pepper, and thyme.
4. Cover and simmer on low heat for 5 hours, stirring occasionally.
5. Stir in remaining 2 tbsp butter before serving

Calories per serving: 620 kcal
Protein: 52g | **Fat:** 44g | **Carbs:** 0g

Organ Meats Like Liver And Heart For Essential Vitamins

Pan-Seared Beef Liver with Garlic Butter

 25 Minutes 2

Ingredients:
- ½ lb beef liver (sliced into thin strips)
- 3 tbsp butter (for cooking and richness)
- ½ tsp sea salt (enhances taste)
- ½ tsp black pepper (for balance)
- 1 garlic clove, minced (adds aroma)
- 1 tbsp lemon juice (for brightness)

Instructions:
1. Rinse beef liver under cold water and pat dry.
2. (Optional) Soak in lemon water for 30 minutes to reduce bitterness.
3. Melt 2 tbsp butter in a skillet over medium heat.
4. Sear liver slices for 25 minutes, flipping once.
5. Stir in remaining butter, garlic, and lemon juice.
6. Sauté for another 30 seconds, then serve warm.

Calories per serving: 450 kcal
Protein: 40g | **Fat:** 30g | **Carbs:** 0g

Slow-Cooked Lamb Heart Stew

 3.5 hours 4

Ingredients:
- 2 lamb hearts (trimmed and diced)
- 3 tbsp butter (for cooking)
- 2 cups bone broth (adds moisture and collagen)
- ½ cup diced onions (for sweetness)
- ½ tsp sea salt (enhances taste)
- ½ tsp black pepper (for balance)
- ½ tsp dried rosemary (for aroma)

Instructions:
1. Melt 1 tbsp butter in a pot over medium heat.
2. Brown heart pieces for 4-5 minutes, stirring occasionally.
3. Add bone broth, onions, and seasonings.
4. Cover and simmer on low heat for 3.5 hours, stirring occasionally.
5. Stir in remaining butter before serving warm.

Calories per serving: 450 kcal
Protein: 48g | **Fat:** 30g | **Carbs:** 0g

Creamy Chicken Liver Pâté

 30 Minutes   4

Ingredients:
- 1 lb chicken livers (trimmed)
- 3 tbsp butter (for cooking)
- ½ cup heavy cream (for creaminess)
- ½ tsp sea salt (enhances taste)
- ½ tsp black pepper (for mild spice)
- ½ tsp dried thyme (for aroma)
- 1 tbsp lemon juice (for freshness)

Instructions:
1. Melt 2 tbsp butter in a pan over medium heat.
2. Add livers and cook for 30 minutes, flipping once.
3. Transfer to a blender or food processor.
4. Add heavy cream, salt, black pepper, thyme, and lemon juice, then blend until smooth.
5. Refrigerate for 2 hours, then serve as a spread or dip.

Calories per serving:420 kcal
Protein: 45g | **Fat:** 30g | **Carbs:** 0g

Grilled Beef Heart Skewers

 20 Minutes   2

Ingredients:
- 1 beef heart (trimmed and cut into cubes)
- 2 tbsp butter (for brushing)
- ½ tsp sea salt (enhances taste)
- ½ tsp black pepper (for balance)
- ½ tsp garlic powder (adds depth)

Instructions:
1. Toss heart cubes with salt, pepper, and garlic powder.
2. Thread onto skewers and grill over medium-high heat for 10 minutes per side.
3. Brush with melted butter before serving warm.

Calories per serving: 480 kcal
Protein: 50g | **Fat:** 32g | **Carbs:** 0g

Pan-Fried Lamb Liver with Onions and Butter

 25 Minutes   2

Ingredients:
- ½ lb lamb liver
- 2 tbsp butter
- ½ cup onions, thinly sliced
- ½ tsp sea salt (enhances flavor)
- ½ tsp black pepper (mild spice)
- 1 tbsp lemon juice

Instructions:
1. Rinse lamb liver under cold water, pat dry, and slice into thin strips.
2. (Optional) Soak in lemon water for 20 minutes to remove any bitterness.
3. Heat 1 tbsp butter in a skillet over medium heat.
4. Add onions and cook for 3-4 minutes until softened.
5. Push onions to the side, add remaining butter, and sear liver for 25 minutes.
6. Drizzle with lemon juice, stir everything together, and serve warm.

Calories per serving: 430 kcal
Protein: 50g | **Fat:** 30g | **Carbs:** 0g

Slow-Cooked Beef Kidney Stew

 3 hours   4

Ingredients:
- 1 lb beef kidney (trimmed and diced)
- 3 tbsp butter (for cooking)
- 2 cups bone broth (adds depth and nutrients)
- ½ cup diced onions
- ½ tsp sea salt (enhances taste)
- ½ tsp black pepper (for balance)
- ½ tsp dried thyme (for aroma)

Instructions:
1. Rinse beef kidney under cold water and pat dry.
2. Cut into bite-sized pieces.
3. Melt 1 tbsp butter in a pot over medium heat.
4. Brown kidney pieces for 4-5 minutes, stirring occasionally.
5. Add bone broth, onions, salt, pepper, and thyme.
6. Cover and simmer on low heat for 3 hours, stirring occasionally.
7. Stir in remaining butter before serving for added richness.

Calories per serving: 440 kcal
Protein: 48g | **Fat:** 28g | **Carbs:** 0g

Braised Pork Heart in Butter and Garlic

⏰ 3.5 hours   🍽 4

Ingredients:
- 2 pork hearts (trimmed and sliced)
- 3 tbsp butter (for richness)
- 2 cups bone broth (adds moisture)
- ½ cup diced onions (for sweetness)
- ½ tsp sea salt (enhances flavor)
- ½ tsp black pepper (for mild spice)
- 1 garlic clove, minced (adds aroma)

Instructions:
1. Melt 1 tbsp butter in a pot over medium heat.
2. Brown pork heart pieces for 5 minutes, stirring occasionally.
3. Add bone broth, onions, salt, pepper, and garlic.
4. Cover and simmer on low heat for 3.5 hours, stirring occasionally.
5. Stir in remaining butter before serving for extra flavor.

Calories per serving: 460 kcal
Protein: 50g | **Fat:** 30g | **Carbs:** 0g

49

Crispy Pan-Fried Beef Spleen with Butter

⏰ 20 Minutes   🍽 2

Ingredients:
- ½ lb beef spleen (sliced into thin strips)
- 3 tbsp butter (for frying and richness)
- ½ tsp sea salt (enhances taste)
- ½ tsp black pepper (for mild spice)
- ½ tsp garlic powder (for depth)

Instructions:
1. Rinse beef spleen under cold water and pat dry.
2. Slice into thin strips for quick cooking.
3. Heat 2 tbsp butter in a pan over medium-high heat.
4. Fry spleen strips for 10 minutes per side, flipping once.
5. Sprinkle with sea salt and black pepper and serve hot.

Calories per serving: 420 kcal
Protein: 48g | **Fat:** 28g | **Carbs:** 0g

Butter-Braised Chicken Gizzards

 1.5 hours 4

Ingredients:
- 1 lb chicken gizzards (trimmed)
- 3 tbsp butter (for cooking)
- 2 cups bone broth (for tenderness)
- ½ tsp sea salt (enhances taste)
- ½ tsp black pepper (for balance)
- ½ tsp dried oregano (for aroma)

Instructions:
1. Heat 1 tbsp butter in a pot over medium heat.
2. Brown gizzards for 5 minutes, stirring occasionally.
3. Add bone broth, salt, pepper, and oregano.
4. Cover and simmer on low heat for 1.5 hours, stirring occasionally.
5. Stir in remaining butter before serving warm.

Calories per serving: 430 kcal
Protein: 46g | **Fat:** 28g | **Carbs:** 0g

Beef Tongue in Butter and Garlic Sauce

 2 hours 4

Ingredients:
- 1 beef tongue (trimmed and cleaned)
- 3 tbsp butter (for basting and richness)
- 2 cups bone broth (for slow cooking)
- ½ tsp sea salt (enhances taste)
- ½ tsp black pepper (for balance)
- 1 garlic clove, minced (adds aroma)
- ½ tsp smoked paprika (for depth)

Instructions:
1. Place beef tongue in a pot, add bone broth, salt, pepper, garlic, and paprika.
2. Cover and simmer on low heat for 2 hours, flipping occasionally.
3. Remove tongue, peel off outer layer, and slice into thin strips.
4. Melt butter in a pan over medium heat.
5. Sear tongue slices for 1-2 minutes per side.
6. Drizzle with extra butter sauce before serving.

Calories per serving: 620 kcal
Protein: 50g | **Fat:** 42g | **Carbs:** 0g

Section D: Quick and Simple Dishes

10-Minute Meals for the Less Enthusiastic Cooks

This section is perfect for those who want to eat well without spending hours in the kitchen. Whether you're short on time, low on energy, or just not a fan of complicated cooking, these 10-minute meals deliver quick nourishment without sacrificing flavor or nutrition. Each recipe is designed to be fuss-free and efficient, making them ideal for seniors who may prefer minimal prep and cleanup. With these speedy dishes, you can enjoy hearty, satisfying meals—even on your laziest days.

5-Ingredient Recipes for Simplicity

Keeping it simple has never tasted so good. This section focuses on recipes made with just five ingredients, proving that less really can be more. Perfect for those who don't want to juggle a long grocery list, these dishes are easy to follow, easy to shop for, and easy to love. Seniors will especially appreciate the streamlined approach, as it reduces both prep time and kitchen stress. Despite the simplicity, each recipe is packed with flavor, nourishment, and carnivore-approved goodness.

10-Minute Meals for the Less Enthusiastic Cooks

Carnivore Deviled Eggs with Beef Bacon Bits

 10 Minutes 2

Ingredients:
- 4 large eggs (boiled and halved)
- 2 tbsp butter (for richness)
- 2 tbsp beef bacon bits
- ½ tsp sea salt (enhances taste)
- ½ tsp black pepper (for mild spice)
- ½ tsp smoked paprika
- 1 tsp Dijon mustard (adds a slight tang)
- 1 tbsp heavy cream (for creaminess)

Instructions:
1. Boil eggs for 7 minutes, then cool, peel, and halve them.
2. Scoop yolks into a bowl and mash with butter, salt, pepper, paprika, mustard, and cream until smooth.
3. Spoon mixture back into egg whites.
4. Top with crispy beef bacon bits and serve immediately.

Calories per serving:480 kcal
Protein: 40g | Fat: 34g | Carbs: 0g

Cheesy Beef & Egg Roll-Ups

 10 Minutes 2

Ingredients:
- ½ lb ground beef
- 2 large eggs (acts as the wrap)
- 2 tbsp butter (for frying)
- ¼ cup shredded cheese ½ tsp sea salt ½ tsp black pepper
- ½ tsp garlic powder (adds depth)

Instructions:
1. Heat 1 tbsp butter in a skillet over medium-high heat.
2. Cook ground beef with salt, black pepper, and garlic powder for 5 minutes, stirring occasionally.
3. In a separate pan, melt the remaining butter and cook whisked eggs for 3 minutes. Flip and cook for another minute.
4. Fill each egg wrap with cooked beef and shredded cheese.

Calories per serving: 520 kcal
Protein: 48g | Fat: 36g | Carbs: 0g

Buttered Scrambled Eggs with Beef Tallow

 5 Minutes 2

Ingredients:
- 4 large eggs
- 2 tbsp beef tallow (adds extra flavor) ½ tsp sea salt (enhances taste)
- ½ tsp black pepper (for balance)
- ½ tsp garlic powder (adds depth)

Instructions:
1. In a bowl, mix eggs, sea salt, black pepper, and garlic powder.
2. Heat beef tallow in a pan over medium-low heat.
3. Pour in egg mixture and cook slowly, stirring continuously for 5 minutes.
4. Plate and enjoy warm.

Calories per serving: 410 kcal
Protein: 34g | **Fat:** 30g | **Carbs:** 0g

Beef & Egg Bowl with Butter Drizzle

 10 Minutes 2

Ingredients:
- ½ lb ground beef
- 2 large eggs
- 2 tbsp butter (for richness)
- ½ tsp sea salt (enhances taste)
- ½ tsp black pepper (for balance)
- ½ tsp smoked paprika (adds warmth)

Instructions:
1. Heat 1 tbsp butter in a skillet over medium-high heat.
2. Brown ground beef for 5-6 minutes, stirring occasionally.
3. Push the beef to one side and crack in eggs.
4. Fry for 3 minutes, or until the yolks are set.
5. Transfer to a bowl and drizzle with remaining butter.

Calories per serving: 500 kcal
Protein: 48g | **Fat:** 32g | **Carbs:** 0g

Carnivore Burger Buns (Meat-Based & Zero-Carb)

 10 Minutes   2

Ingredients:
- ½ lb ground chicken or ground beef (for structure)
- 1 large egg (acts as a binder)
- 2 tbsp grated Parmesan cheese
- 1 tbsp butter or beef tallow
- ½ tsp sea salt (enhances taste)
- ½ tsp black pepper (for mild spice)
- ½ tsp garlic powder

Instructions:
1. In a bowl, mix ground meat, egg, Parmesan cheese, sea salt, black pepper, and garlic powder.
2. Stir until well combined.
3. Divide the mixture into two equal portions and shape into flat, round buns.
4. Heat butter or beef tallow in a skillet over medium heat.
5. Cook each bun for 8 minutes per side, flipping once, until golden brown and firm.
6. Let cool for 1-2 minutes, then use as burger buns with your favorite carnivore fillings like buttered beef patties or fried eggs.

Calories per serving: 320 kcal
Protein: 34g | **Fat:** 22g | **Carbs:** 0g

Butter-Seared Lamb Chops with Garlic and Herbs

 10 Minutes   2

Ingredients:
- 2 small lamb chops
- 2 tbsp butter (for searing)
- ½ tsp sea salt (enhances flavor)
- ½ tsp black pepper (for mild spice)
- ½ tsp garlic powder (adds depth)
- ½ tsp smoked paprika (for warmth)
- ½ tsp dried thyme
- 1 tbsp Worcestershire sauce
- 1 tbsp lemon juice

Instructions:
1. Season lamb chops with salt, pepper, garlic powder, paprika, and thyme.
2. Drizzle Worcestershire sauce over the chops and let sit for 2 minutes.
3. Heat butter in a skillet over medium-high heat.
4. Sear lamb chops for 3-4 minutes per side until browned.
5. Cook until the internal temperature reaches 135°F for medium-rare.
6. Drizzle with lemon juice and let rest for 2 minutes before serving.

Calories per serving: 450 kcal
Protein: 42g | **Fat:** 30g | **Carbs:** 0g

Spicy Butter-Fried Chicken Thighs

⏰ 10 Minutes   🍽 2

Ingredients:
- 2 boneless, skin-on chicken thighs
- 2 tbsp butter (for frying)
- ½ tsp sea salt (enhances taste)
- ½ tsp black pepper (for mild spice)
- ½ tsp smoked paprika (adds smoky warmth)
- ½ tsp cayenne pepper
- ½ tsp garlic powder (adds depth)
- 1 tbsp Dijon mustard (for a tangy bite)
- 1 tbsp Worcestershire sauce (for extra umami)

Instructions:
1. Rub chicken thighs with salt, black pepper, paprika, cayenne, and garlic powder.
2. Coat with Dijon mustard and Worcestershire sauce.
3. Melt butter in a skillet over medium-high heat.
4. Cook chicken for 5 minutes per side, flipping once.
5. Let rest for 1-2 minutes, then serve warm.

Calories per serving: 470 kcal
Protein: 44g | **Fat:** 32g | **Carbs:** 0g

Garlic Butter Shrimp with Lemon and Herbs

⏰ 5 Minutes   🍽 2

Ingredients:
- 1 lb shrimp (peeled and deveined)
- 2 tbsp butter (for richness)
- ½ tsp sea salt (enhances taste)
- ½ tsp black pepper (for mild spice)
- ½ tsp smoked paprika (adds warmth)
- ½ tsp dried oregano (for mild earthiness)
- 2 garlic cloves, minced (adds aroma)
- 1 tbsp lemon juice (for brightness)

Instructions:
1. Toss shrimp with salt, pepper, paprika, oregano, and garlic.
2. Melt butter in a pan over medium-high heat.
3. Add shrimp and cook for 2-3 minutes per side, flipping once.
4. Drizzle with lemon juice before serving.

Calories per serving: 410 kcal
Protein: 48g | **Fat:** 28g | **Carbs:** 0g

Butter-Fried Chicken Liver and Egg Scramble

 10 Minutes   2

Ingredients:
- ½ lb chicken liver (trimmed and chopped into bite-sized pieces)
- 2 large eggs
- 2 tbsp butter
- ½ tsp sea salt (enhances taste)
- ½ tsp black pepper (for mild spice)
- ½ tsp garlic powder (adds depth)
- ½ tsp dried thyme
- 1 tbsp heavy cream

Instructions:
1. Heat 1 tbsp butter in a pan over medium-high heat.
2. Add the liver, season with salt, pepper, garlic powder, and thyme. Cook for 4-5 minutes until browned.
3. Whisk eggs with heavy cream in a bowl.
4. Push liver to one side of the pan. Add remaining butter, then pour in the egg mixture.
5. Scramble gently for 3-4 minutes until eggs are just set.
6. Stir liver and eggs together, then serve hot.

Calories per serving: 490 kcal
Protein: 50g | **Fat:** 34g | **Carbs:** 0g

Cheesy Beef & Butter Chaffle (Carnivore Waffle)

 7 Minutes   2

Ingredients:
- 2 large eggs (acts as a binder)
- ½ cup shredded cheese
- 2 tbsp butter (adds richness)
- ¼ cup cooked ground beef or crumbled bacon (for protein)
- ½ tsp sea salt (enhances taste)
- ½ tsp black pepper (for mild spice)
- ½ tsp garlic powder (for depth)

Instructions:
1. In a bowl, whisk eggs, shredded cheese, salt, black pepper, and garlic powder until well combined.
2. Stir in cooked beef or bacon for extra flavor.
3. Preheat a waffle iron and grease with butter.
4. Pour in half the mixture and cook for 3-4 minutes, or until crispy and golden.
5. Repeat with remaining batter, then serve warm with extra melted butter on top!

Calories per serving: 480 kcal
Protein: 42g | **Fat:** 34g | **Carbs:** 0g

5-Ingredient Recipes For Simplicity

(In this section the main ingredients are only 5, rest are spices and sauces to enhance the flavour)

Spicy Garlic Shrimp

 5 Minutes   2

Ingredients:

- 1 lb large shrimp (peeled and deveined) (450g)
- 2 tbsp butter (30g)
- 3 cloves garlic, minced (10g)
- 1 tsp red pepper flakes (2g)
- Juice of 1 lemon (30ml)
- Paprika: Adds a smoky flavor.
- Cayenne Pepper: For extra heat.
- Chili Oil

Instructions:

1. Melt butter in a skillet over medium heat.
2. Add garlic and red pepper flakes and sauté for 1 minute until fragrant.
3. Toss in shrimp, cooking for 2-3 minutes per side until pink and opaque.
4. Squeeze lemon juice over the shrimp before serving.

Calories per serving: 380 kcal
Protein: 1g | **Fat:** 12g | **Carbs:** 0g

Bacon and Egg Cups

 15 Minutes   2

Ingredients:

- 4 large eggs
- 4 strips of bacon
- ½ tsp sea salt, ½ tsp black pepper, ½ tsp garlic powder
- ½ tsp smoked paprika (adds smokiness)
- ¼ tsp red pepper flakes (adds heat)
- ¼ cup shredded cheese (adds creaminess)

Instructions:

1. Preheat oven to 375°F (190°C).
2. Line a muffin tin with bacon strips, shaping them into cups.
3. Crack an egg into each bacon cup and season with spices.
4. Bake for 12-15 minutes until eggs reach desired doneness.
5. Let cool for 2 minutes before serving warm.

Calories per serving: 410 kcal
Protein: 38g | **Fat:** 30g | **Carbs:** 0g

Honey Soy Glazed Salmon

 10 Minutes 🍴 2

Ingredients:
- 2 salmon fillets (200g each)
- 2 tbsp soy sauce (30ml)
- 2 tbsp honey (40g)
- 1 clove garlic, minced (5g)
- 1 tsp sesame oil (5ml)
- Ginger: Adds a spicy, aromatic flavor.
- Sriracha: For heat.
- Lime Juice: Adds acidity.

Instructions:
1. Mix soy sauce, honey, garlic, and sesame oil in a bowl.
2. Marinate salmon fillets for 10 minutes.
3. Heat a pan over medium heat and cook salmon for 4-5 minutes per side, brushing with remaining glaze.
4. Drizzle extra glaze over salmon before serving.

Calories per serving: 400 kcal
Protein: 12g | **Fat:** 18g | **Carbs:** 0g

Butter Egg Latte

🕐 15 Minutes 🍴 2

Ingredients:
- 1 large egg
- 1 tbsp unsalted butter (15g)
- 1 cup hot water (240ml)
- ½ tsp ground cinnamon (optional)
- Pinch of sea salt
- ¼ tsp vanilla extract – Adds warmth.
- Pinch of nutmeg or cardamom – For extra spice.
- 1 tbsp heavy cream – Enhances creaminess.

Instructions:
1. **lend:** Combine egg, butter, hot water, cinnamon, and salt in a blender. Blend on high for 30–45 sec until smooth and frothy.
2. **Serve:** Pour into a mug and enjoy hot. Optionally, sprinkle cinnamon or nutmeg on top.

Calories per serving: 210 kcal
Protein: 0g | **Fat:** 18g | **Carbs:** 7g

Lemon Garlic Grilled Chicken

 15 Minutes   2

Ingredients:
- 2 boneless, skinless chicken breasts (250g)
- 2 cloves garlic, minced (5g)
- Juice of 1 lemon (30ml)
- 2 tbsp olive oil (30ml)
- Salt and pepper to taste
- Fresh rosemary or thyme: For an aromatic touch.
- Red pepper flakes: For a hint of heat.
- Soy sauce: For an umami boost.

Instructions:
1. Mix garlic, lemon juice, olive oil, salt, and pepper in a bowl.
2. Marinate chicken breasts for 30 minutes.
3. Grill for 6-7 minutes per side until fully cooked.
4. Let rest for 2 minutes, then serve.

Calories per serving: 280 kcal
Protein: 0g | **Fat:** 15g | **Carbs:** 0g

Carnivore Egg Muffins

 10 Minutes 2

Ingredients:
- 6 large eggs
- ½ cup cooked ground beef or bacon bits (100g)
- ¼ cup shredded cheese (30g)
- 2 tbsp melted butter (30g)
- ½ tsp sea salt (2g)
- Optional: black pepper, smoked paprika, chili flakes

Instructions:
1. Preheat oven to 350°F (175°C) and grease a muffin tin.
2. Whisk eggs, then mix in meat, cheese, butter, salt, and optional spices.
3. Divide evenly into 8 muffin cups (¾ full).
4. Bake for 18–20 min until set and golden.
5. Cool slightly before serving or refrigerate for later.

Calories per serving: 150 kcal
Protein: 11g | **Fat:** 12g | **Carbs:** 0g

Mozzarella-Stuffed Meatballs

⏰ 25 Minutes 🍽 4

Ingredients:
- 1 lb ground beef (450g)
- 4 oz mozzarella cheese, cut into small cubes (113g)
- 1 large egg
- 1 tsp salt
- 1/2 tsp black pepper
- Garlic powder powder: Enhances taste.
- Marinara sauce: For serving.

Instructions:
1. Preheat oven to 400°F (200°C).
2. In a bowl, combine ground beef, egg, salt, pepper, garlic, and onion powder. Mix until combined.
3. Take a portion of meat, flatten it, place a mozzarella cube in the center, and wrap the meat around to seal. Repeat.
4. Place meatballs on a baking sheet and bake for 20-25 minutes until browned and cooked through.
5. Serve hot, optionally with marinara sauce.

Calories per serving: 420 kcal
Protein: 38g | **Fat:** 30g | **Carbs:** 0g

Carnivore Egg-in-a-Hole

⏰ 10 Minutes 🍽 2

Ingredients:
- 1/2 lb ground beef (225g)
- 1 large egg
- 1 tbsp butter
- Salt to taste
- Pepper to taste
- Paprika: For a smoky flavor.
- Hot sauce: Adds heat.
- Cheddar cheese: For extra richness.

Instructions:
1. Shape the ground beef into a patty with a hole in the center (like a donut).
2. Heat butter in a skillet over medium heat. Place the beef patty in the skillet and cook for 3-4 minutes on one side.
3. Flip the patty and crack the egg into the hole. Season with salt and pepper. Cover and cook until the egg reaches your desired doneness.
4. Serve immediately, optionally topped with cheddar cheese or hot sauce.

Calories per serving: 380 kcal
Protein: 35g | **Fat:** 28g | **Carbs:** 0g

Carnivore Stroganoff

 15 Minutes   4

Ingredients:
- 1 lb ground beef (450g)
- 1/2 cup heavy cream (120ml)
- 2 tbsp butter
- Salt to taste
- Pepper to taste
- Garlic powder: Adds depth.
- Onion powder: Enhances flavor.
- Paprika: For color and taste.

Instructions:
1. In a skillet over medium heat, cook the ground beef until browned. Drain excess fat if necessary.
2. Lower the heat and stir in the heavy cream and butter. Season with salt and pepper.
3. Let the mixture simmer for 5 minutes, allowing the sauce to thicken.
4. Serve hot, optionally sprinkled with paprika.

Calories per serving: 450 kcal
Protein: 36g | **Fat:** 34g | **Carbs:** 0g

Bacon-Wrapped Chicken Tenders

 25 Minutes   2

Ingredients:
- 4 chicken tenders (300g total)
- 4 strips of bacon
- 1 tsp sea salt (5g)
- ½ tsp black pepper (2g)
- ½ tsp smoked paprika (2g)
- Garlic powder (½ tsp): Enhances depth of flavor.
- Cayenne pepper (¼ tsp)
- Dijon mustard (1 tbsp)

Instructions:
1. Preheat oven to 400°F (200°C).
2. Season chicken tenders with salt, black pepper, and smoked paprika.
3. Wrap each tender tightly with one strip of bacon, securing the ends if needed.
4. Place on a baking sheet lined with parchment paper.
5. Bake for 20-25 minutes, flipping halfway through, until bacon is crispy and chicken is fully cooked.
6. Let rest for 2 minutes before serving.

Calories per serving: 450 kcal
Protein: 48g | **Fat:** 28g | **Carbs:** 0g

Chapter 4: Adapting to Common Age-Related Challenges

1- Overcoming Constipation Without Fibers

Constipation is a common concern among seniors, often attributed to slowed digestion and reduced physical activity. Conventional wisdom suggests increasing fiber intake, but for those following a carnivore diet, fiber isn't necessary for optimal gut health. Instead, focusing on hydration, healthy fats, and essential minerals can effectively relieve constipation without the bloating and discomfort that fiber sometimes causes.

1. 'Prioritize Hydration'
Dehydration is one of the leading causes of constipation. Seniors should aim to drink adequate water throughout the day, ideally paired with electrolytes like sodium, potassium, and magnesium to maintain fluid balance. Bone broth is an excellent choice, as it replenishes minerals while keeping digestion smooth.

2. 'Increase Healthy Fats'
Fats act as natural lubricants for the digestive system. Adding butter, tallow, bone marrow, and fatty cuts of meat to meals helps promote softer stools and easier elimination. These fats also encourage the production of bile, which further aids digestion

3. 'Consume Collagen and Gelatin'
Collagen-rich foods like bone broth, slow-cooked meats, and gelatin support gut lining health and improve motility. They help maintain a smooth, well-functioning digestive tract without relying on fiber.

2- Strategies to Prevent Nutritional Deficiencies

As we age, the body's ability to absorb and utilize essential nutrients declines, making it crucial to adopt strategies that ensure **optimal nutrition**. While the **carnivore diet naturally provides bioavailable vitamins and minerals**, seniors must be mindful of potential deficiencies. Here's how to maintain a well-balanced diet while preventing common nutrient shortfalls:

1. 'Prioritize Organ Meats for Maximum Nutrition'
Organ meats, such as **liver, heart, and kidney**, are nature's multivitamins. **Liver is rich in vitamin A, B12, iron, and folate**, essential for **energy, brain function, and immune support**. Including **3-4 servings of organ meats per week** can prevent deficiencies in critical nutrients that are harder to obtain from muscle meats alone.

2. 'Incorporate Collagen and Bone Broth for Joint and Gut Health'
Collagen, found in **bone broth, tendons, and skin-on meats**, provides **glycine, proline, and other amino acids** that support **joint flexibility, digestion, and skin elasticity**. Regular consumption of **bone broth or gelatin** can help prevent **joint pain, brittle nails, and digestive issues**.

3. 'Ensure Adequate Fat Intake for Vitamin Absorption'
Fat-soluble vitamins (**A, D, E, and K2**) require dietary fat for proper absorption. Eating **fatty cuts of meat, bone marrow, butter, and egg yolks** ensures that the body can effectively absorb these essential nutrients. **Grass-fed butter and animal fats** also provide **butyrate and CLA**, which support **gut health and inflammation control**.

4. 'Optimize Electrolytes and Minerals'

Sodium, potassium, and magnesium play a vital role in **hydration, nerve function, and muscle contraction**. A carnivore diet is naturally low in plant-based sources of these minerals, so seniors should **prioritize salt, bone broth, and mineral-rich meats**. Supplementing **magnesium glycinate** can help prevent cramps, fatigue, and sluggish digestion.

3- Adjustments for Those with Chewing Difficulties or Digestive Issues

As we age, chewing strength and digestive efficiency can decline, making it difficult to consume and process tougher cuts of meat. However, with the right adjustments, seniors can still enjoy the **nutrient-rich benefits of a carnivore diet** while ensuring easy digestion and minimal discomfort.

1. 'Opt for Tender, Slow-Cooked Meats'

Tough cuts of meat, such as **brisket, short ribs, and shank**, become **soft and easy to chew** when slow-cooked. Cooking meats in a **slow cooker, pressure cooker, or braising them in bone broth** for several hours **breaks down connective tissue**, making them more digestible and gentler on teeth and gums.

2. Choose Ground and Minced Meats

Ground meats, such as **ground beef, lamb, and turkey**, require **less chewing effort** while still delivering high-quality protein. Preparing **soft-textured meals like meatballs, patties, or minced meat cooked in butter** makes eating easier while maintaining **optimal nutrition**.

3. 'Incorporate Soft and Gelatinous Cuts'

Cuts like **oxtail, marrow bones, and chicken feet** contain **collagen and gelatin**, which support **joint health and gut lining repair**. These cuts cook into **soft, easily digestible textures** and can be blended into **soups and stews** for added nourishment.

4. 'Use Bone Broth and Blended Meat-Based Soups'

For those struggling with **both chewing and digestion, bone broth, pureed meat soups, and blended organ meats** provide **highly bioavailable nutrients** without requiring extensive chewing. **Beef liver pâté** or **blended bone marrow soups** are excellent ways to increase **vitamins and minerals** in a **smooth, easy-to-swallow form**.

4- Adapting to Fat Digestion Problems for Those with Gallbladder or Liver Issues

For individuals with gallbladder or liver issues, digesting high amounts of fat can be challenging. Since the carnivore diet relies heavily on healthy animal fats, proper adjustments can help ease digestion, prevent discomfort, and ensure optimal nutrient absorption.

1. 'Start with Leaner Cuts and Gradually Increase Fats'

Those struggling with fat digestion should begin with leaner meats, such as chicken breast, sirloin, and lean ground beef, before gradually introducing fattier cuts. This allows the digestive system to adjust without overwhelming the liver or gallbladder.

2. 'Incorporate Digestive Aids for Fat Breakdown'

The gallbladder stores and releases bile, which is essential for breaking down fats. Without it, or in cases of reduced liver function, bile production can be insufficient, leading to bloating or discomfort. To support fat digestion:

- Take ox bile supplements to mimic natural bile function.
- Include apple cider vinegar or lemon juice before meals to stimulate bile flow.
- Drink warm bone broth to support digestive enzyme production.

3. 'Eat Smaller, More Frequent Meals'

Instead of consuming large fatty meals, seniors with fat digestion issues may benefit from smaller, more frequent portions. This prevents overloading the liver and gallbladder, allowing the body to process fats more efficiently.

4. 'Prioritize Easily Digestible Fats'

Certain fats are easier to digest than others. Instead of heavy rendered fats, opt for:

- Butter or ghee – Contains minimal lactose and is gentle on digestion.
- Bone marrow – Packed with nutrients and easier to absorb.
- Fatty fish like salmon and sardines – High in omega-3s, which support liver function.

Chapter 5: Meal Planning and Shopping Made Easy

120-Day Detailed Meal Plan

Day	Breakfast	Lunch	Dinner	Snacks
1	Scrambled eggs with butter and bone broth	Slow-cooked beef shank with bone broth	Tender slow-braised oxtail	Bone marrow spread on beef jerky
2	Pan-seared salmon with butter	Ground beef stir-fry with butter	Pan-seared beef liver with butter	Hard-boiled eggs with butter dip
3	Beef liver sautéed in ghee	Pan-seared chicken thighs with bone broth	Pork ribs slow-cooked in tallow	Beef liver pâté with tallow crisps
4	Ground beef patties cooked in tallow	Beef heart stir-fry with tallow	Crispy sardines in butter	Pork rinds dipped in beef tallow
5	Cheesy omelet with bone marrow	Grilled pork belly	Bone-in ribeye with garlic butter	Cheese cubes with bone broth sip
6	Air-fried lamb chops with butter	Butter-basted ribeye steak	Chicken drumsticks cooked in beef fat	Smoked salmon slices with butter
7	Hard-boiled eggs dipped in beef fat	Carnivore beef stew with bone marrow	Grass-fed burger patties with bone broth	Air-fried beef fat trimmings
8	Pork belly slices pan-fried in butter	Air-fried salmon fillet	Slow-cooked lamb shoulder	Carnivore meat chips (dried steak)
9	Chicken drumsticks cooked in beef fat	Grass-fed burger patties with bone broth	Air-fried beef steak strips	Cold beef tongue slices with salt
10	Scrambled eggs with butter and bone broth	Slow-cooked beef shank with bone broth	Tender slow-braised oxtail	Bone marrow spread on beef jerky
11	Pan-seared salmon with butter	Ground beef stir-fry with butter	Pan-seared beef liver with butter	Hard-boiled eggs with butter dip
12	Beef liver sautéed in ghee	Pan-seared chicken thighs with bone broth	Pork ribs slow-cooked in tallow	Beef liver pâté with tallow crisps
13	Ground beef patties cooked in tallow	Beef heart stir-fry with tallow	Crispy sardines in butter	Pork rinds dipped in beef tallow
14	Cheesy omelet with bone marrow	Grilled pork belly slices	Bone-in ribeye with garlic butter	Cheese cubes with bone broth sip
15	Air-fried lamb chops with butter	Butter-basted ribeye steak	Chicken drumsticks cooked in beef fat	Smoked salmon slices with butter
17	Hard-boiled eggs dipped in beef fat	Carnivore beef stew with bone marrow	Grass-fed burger patties with bone broth	Air-fried beef fat trimmings

18	Pork belly slices pan-fried in butter	Air-fried salmon	Slow-cooked lamb shoulder	Carnivore meat chips (dried steak)
19	Chicken drumsticks cooked in beef fat	Grass-fed burger patties with bone broth	Air-fried beef steak strips	Cold beef tongue slices with salt
20	Crispy sardines in butter	Slow-cooked lamb shoulder	Beef tongue braised in bone broth	Chicken skin crisps fried in ghee
21	Scrambled eggs with butter and bone broth	Slow-cooked beef shank with bone broth	Tender slow-braised oxtail	Bone marrow spread on beef jerky
22	Pan-seared salmon with butter	Ground beef stir-fry with butter	Pan-seared beef liver with butter	Hard-boiled eggs with butter dip
23	Beef liver sautéed in ghee	Pan-seared chicken thighs with bone broth	Pork ribs slow-cooked in tallow	Beef liver pâté with tallow crisps
24	Ground beef patties cooked in tallow	Beef heart stir-fry with tallow	Crispy sardines in butter	Pork rinds dipped in beef tallow
25	Lamb sweetbreads & bone marrow	Rabbit stew	BBQ lamb leg	Beef liver chips
26	Scrambled duck eggs & pork strips	Elk tenderloin steak	Pan-fried catfish fillets	Hard cheese cubes (optional)
27	Chicken hearts stir-fried	Roasted pork ribs	Braised beef cheeks	Tuna jerky
28	Bone marrow & boiled eggs	Smoked mackerel steaks	Duck breast grilled	Sardine pate
29	Pork cracklings & duck eggs	Venison kebabs	Turkey thighs roasted	Beef tendon crisps
30	Ribeye steak & scrambled eggs	Pan-seared salmon	Grilled rabbit legs	Pork skin chips
31	Chicken liver fried in butter	Smoked trout fillets	BBQ pork belly	Biltong slices
32	Ribeye steak & scrambled eggs	Pan-seared salmon	Grilled rabbit legs	Pork skin chips
33	Chicken liver fried in butter	Smoked trout fillets	BBQ pork belly	Biltong slices
32	Venison sausages & eggs	Lamb riblets grilled	Beef ribs slow-roasted	Biltong slices
33	Bone marrow & duck eggs	Rabbit liver & heart fry	Pan-seared swordfish (optional)	Beef cracklings
34	Beef heart & scrambled eggs	Roast goose breast	Grilled turkey legs	Chicken skins crisps
	Pork sausages & bone marrow	Smoked bison sausages	BBQ lamb chops	Sardine pate

36	Venison liver fried in tallow	Roasted Cornish hen	Pan-fried salmon steaks	Beef jerky sticks
37	Ribeye steak bites & egg yolks	Grilled elk steaks	Crispy pork belly roast	Turkey cracklings
38	Bone broth & pork belly	Duck breast seared	Slow-cooked beef oxtail	Chicken skin chips
39	Crispy sardines in butter	Slow-cooked lamb shoulder	Beef tongue braised in bone broth	Chicken skin crisps fried in ghee
40	Scrambled eggs with butter and bone broth	Slow-cooked beef shank with bone broth	Tender slow-braised oxtail	Bone marrow spread on beef jerky
41	Pan-seared salmon with butter	Ground beef stir-fry with butter	Pan-seared beef liver with butter	Hard-boiled eggs with butter dip
42	Beef liver sautéed in ghee	Pan-seared chicken thighs with bone broth	Pork ribs slow-cooked in tallow	Beef liver pâté with tallow crisps
43	Ground beef patties cooked in tallow	Beef heart stir-fry with tallow	Crispy sardines in butter	Pork rinds dipped in beef tallow
44	Cheesy omelet with bone marrow	Grilled pork belly slices	Bone-in ribeye with garlic butter	Cheese cubes with bone broth sip
45	Air-fried lamb chops with butter	Butter-basted ribeye steak	Chicken drumsticks cooked in beef fat	Smoked salmon slices with butter
46	Hard-boiled eggs dipped in beef fat	Carnivore beef stew with bone marrow	Grass-fed burger patties with bone broth	Air-fried beef fat trimmings
47	Pork belly slices pan-fried in butter	Air-fried salmon fillet	Slow-cooked lamb shoulder	Carnivore meat chips (dried steak)
48	Ribeye steak & bone marrow	Grilled lamb chops	Roasted duck leg	Beef jerky
49	Chicken drumsticks cooked in beef fat	Grass-fed burger patties with bone broth	Air-fried beef steak strips	Cold beef tongue slices with salt
50	Crispy sardines in butter	Slow-cooked lamb shoulder	Beef tongue braised in bone broth	Chicken skin crisps fried in ghee
51	Scrambled eggs with butter and bone broth	Slow-cooked beef shank with bone broth	Tender slow-braised oxtail	Bone marrow spread on beef jerky
52	Pan-seared salmon with butter	Ground beef stir-fry with butter	Pan-seared beef liver with butter	Hard-boiled eggs with butter dip
53	Beef liver sautéed in ghee	Pan-seared chicken thighs with bone broth	Pork ribs slow-cooked in tallow	Beef liver pâté with tallow crisps
54	Ground beef patties cooked in tallow	Beef heart stir-fry with tallow	Crispy sardines in butter	Pork rinds dipped in beef tallow
55	Cheesy omelet with bone marrow	Grilled pork belly slices	Bone-in ribeye with garlic butter	Cheese cubes with bone broth sip

56	Air-fried lamb chops with butter	Butter-basted ribeye steak	Chicken drumsticks cooked in beef fat	Smoked salmon slices with butter
57	Hard-boiled eggs dipped in beef fat	Carnivore beef stew with bone marrow	Grass-fed burger patties with bone broth	Air-fried beef fat trimmings
58	Pork belly slices pan-fried in butter	Air-fried salmon fillet	Slow-cooked lamb shoulder	Carnivore meat chips (dried steak)
59	Chicken drumsticks cooked in beef fat	Grass-fed burger patties with bone broth	Air-fried beef steak strips	Cold beef tongue slices with salt
60	Crispy sardines in butter	Slow-cooked lamb shoulder	Beef tongue braised in bone broth	Chicken skin crisps fried in ghee
61	Scrambled eggs with butter and bone broth	Slow-cooked beef shank with bone broth	Tender slow-braised oxtail	Bone marrow spread on beef jerky
62	Pan-seared salmon with butter	Ground beef stir-fry with butter	Pan-seared beef liver with butter	Hard-boiled eggs with butter dip
63	Beef liver sautéed in ghee	Pan-seared chicken thighs with bone broth	Pork ribs slow-cooked in tallow	Beef liver pâté with tallow crisps
64	Ground beef patties cooked in tallow	Beef heart stir-fry with tallow	Crispy sardines in butter	Pork rinds dipped in beef tallow
65	Cheesy omelet with bone marrow	Grilled pork belly slices	Bone-in ribeye with garlic butter	Cheese cubes with bone broth sip
66	Air-fried lamb chops with butter	Butter-basted ribeye steak	Chicken drumsticks cooked in beef fat	Smoked salmon slices with butter
67	Hard-boiled eggs dipped in beef fat	Carnivore beef stew with bone marrow	Grass-fed burger patties with bone broth	Air-fried beef fat trimmings
68	Pork belly slices pan-fried in butter	Air-fried salmon fillet	Slow-cooked lamb shoulder	Carnivore meat chips (dried steak)
69	Chicken drumsticks cooked in beef fat	Grass-fed burger patties with bone broth	Air-fried beef steak strips	Cold beef tongue slices with salt
70	Crispy sardines in butter	Slow-cooked lamb shoulder	Beef tongue braised in bone broth	Chicken skin crisps fried in ghee
71	Scrambled eggs with butter and bone broth	Slow-cooked beef shank with bone broth	Tender slow-braised oxtail	Bone marrow spread on beef jerky
72	Pan-seared salmon with butter	Ground beef stir-fry with butter	Pan-seared beef liver with butter	Hard-boiled eggs with butter dip
73	Ribeye steak & bone marrow	Grilled lamb chops	Roasted duck leg	Beef jerky
74	Scrambled eggs in beef tallow	Pork belly slices	Grilled salmon with skin	Hard-boiled quail eggs

75	Beef liver & bacon	Turkey breast cutlets	Grass-fed ground beef pattie	Pork rinds
76	Duck eggs fried in lard	Grilled venison steaks	Pan-seared chicken thighs	Smoked salmon slices
77	Pork sausages & soft-boiled eggs	Lamb heart skewers	Crispy pork skin & roasted pork shoulder	Biltong
78	Omelet with chicken hearts	Sardines in olive oil	BBQ short ribs	Bone broth gelatin cubes
79	Fried goat cheese (if tolerated) & bacon	Chicken stew	Grilled bison steak	Boiled chicken eggs
80	Beef kidney sautéed in butter	Roasted chicken wings	Pan-fried trout with skin	Pepperoni slices
81	Venison sausages & scrambled eggs	Smoked pork hocks	Lamb ribs baked in tallow	Anchovies
82	Chicken liver pate & pork cracklings	Pan-fried cod	Roasted guinea fowl	Beef bone broth cup
83	Bone marrow & boiled eggs	Grilled elk steak	Crispy duck breast	Turkey jerky
84	Lamb liver & sweetbreads	Bacon-wrapped chicken drumsticks	Pan-fried catfish	Pork belly bites
85	Ground pork & scrambled duck eggs	Grilled chicken thighs	Slow-cooked beef shank	Sardine fillets
86	Venison bacon & fried eggs	Bison meatballs	Crispy pork belly cubes	Chicken skin crisps
87	Pan-fried sweetbreads	Roast wild boar	Pan-seared mackerel	Hard cheese cubes (optional)
88	Ribeye steak bites & egg yolks	Turkey hearts stew	Roasted Cornish hen	Pork cracklings
89	Scrambled quail eggs & bacon	Baked salmon collar	Venison chops with bone marrow butter	Boiled beef tendons
90	Pan-fried calf liver	Chicken gizzards stir-fried	Grilled duck legs	Smoked trout fillet
91	Beef heart hash & eggs	Sardines in pork fat	BBQ lamb shank	Egg yolk bombs
92	Pork liver sausages & eggs	Rabbit liver pate	Roast turkey thighs	Cold shrimp (peeled)
93	Bone broth & beef ribs	Lamb kidneys grilled	Grilled swordfish (if tolerated)	Jerky crisps
94	Smoked salmon & scrambled eggs	Veal cutlets	Roast duck leg quarters	Chicken cracklings

95	Duck fat fried eggs & sausage	Venison stew	Seared tuna steaks (optional)	Hard-boiled goose eggs
96	Lamb liver & kidney fry	Baked Cornish hen drumsticks	Pork tenderloin roast	Beef tendon crisps
97	Ribeye strips & marrow bones	Grilled sardines	Rabbit leg stew	Dried beef liver snacks
98	Poached duck eggs & bacon	Elk burgers	Crispy skin pork belly	Turkey meat sticks
99	Chicken hearts & gizzards	Smoked mackerel fillet	BBQ ribs (beef or pork)	Pork cracklings
100	Calf sweetbreads pan-fried	Smoked mackerel fillet	BBQ ribs (beef or pork)	Pork cracklings
101	Calf sweetbreads pan-fried	Duck breast slices	Bison sirloin steak	Sardine pate (home-made)
102	Pork sausage patties & eggs	Lamb ribs grilled	Slow-cooked ox tail	Salmon jerky
103	Beef fat fried eggs & bacon	Pan-fried trout fillet	Roasted quail	Chicken skin chips
104	Grilled lamb liver & marrow	Turkey liver & hearts stew	Pork ribs slow-cooked in lard	Dried anchovies
105	Venison bacon & scrambled eggs	Chicken wings in duck fat	Beef chuck roast	Boiled turkey eggs
106	Bone marrow & scrambled duck eggs	Rabbit confit	Pan-fried salmon belly	Pork belly crisps
107	Chicken liver omelet	Rabbit confit	Pan-fried salmon belly	Pork belly crisps
108	Chicken liver omelet	BBQ bison ribs	Crispy roast duck thighs	Hard goat cheese (optional)
109	Beef tongue slices & eggs	Smoked pork loin	Slow-cooked lamb shoulder	Beef jerky sticks
110	Pan-seared veal liver	Chicken leg quarters roasted	Grilled tuna steaks	Pork fat trimmings
111	Pork cracklings & boiled eggs	Grilled elk medallions	Roast goose leg	Turkey cracklings
112	Scrambled quail eggs & lamb bacon	Smoked trout	Braised pork cheeks	Bone broth gummies
113	Ribeye strips & bone marrow	Grilled rabbit saddle	BBQ short ribs (beef)	Bone broth gummies
114	Ribeye strips & bone marrow	Grilled rabbit saddle	BBQ short ribs (beef)	Sardine fillets

115	Duck egg omelet & pork belly	Turkey burgers	Grilled lamb steaks	Biltong slices
116	Chicken gizzards fried in tallow	Venison roast	Pan-fried salmon steaks	Beef cracklings
117	Pork sausage links & eggs	Grilled lamb hearts	Roasted wild duck	Turkey jerky
118	Beef liver with bacon	Grilled sardines	BBQ pork shoulder	Smoked salmon cubes
119	Venison jerky & scrambled eggs	Roasted turkey wings	Slow-cooked beef brisket	Pork belly strips
120	Duck leg confit & eggs	Pan-fried trout fillets	Bison ribeye steak	Chicken skins crisps

Simplified Shopping Lists to Keep You Organized

Maintaining a carnivore diet long-term is much easier when you have an organized shopping list. By breaking your list into categories, you can ensure you always have the right ingredients on hand, reducing meal prep stress and making shopping trips quick and efficient.

1. 'Essential Proteins (Core of the Diet)'
These are the foundation of your meals, providing high-quality protein and healthy fats for energy and muscle maintenance.

'Beef Cuts': 'Ribeye, sirloin, brisket, short ribs, oxtail, ground beef, beef shank'
'Pork Cuts': 'Pork belly, pork chops, pork ribs, ground pork'
'Lamb & Goat': 'Lamb chops, lamb shoulder, ground lamb'
'Poultry': 'Whole chicken, chicken thighs, chicken wings, turkey thighs'
'Seafood': 'Salmon, sardines, mackerel, cod, shrimp, scallops'
'Organ Meats': 'Beef liver, beef heart, kidney, bone marrow, beef tongue'

2. 'Fats for Cooking and Nutrition'
Healthy fats are crucial for energy, hormone balance, and digestion.

Animal-Based Fats: 'Grass-fed butter, ghee, beef tallow, pork lard, duck fat'
Fatty Meats: 'Ribeye, pork belly, bone marrow, salmon, sardines'
Eggs: 'Whole eggs with yolk (pasture-raised preferred)'

3. 'Bone Broth and Collagen Sources'
Bone broth and collagen-rich foods support joint health, digestion, and skin elasticity.

'Bones for Broth': 'Beef marrow bones, oxtail, chicken feet, knuckle bones'
'Collagen-Rich Cuts': 'Beef shank, lamb neck, slow-cooked tendons'

4. 'Hydration and Electrolytes'
Electrolyte balance is key for preventing muscle cramps, fatigue, and dehydration.

'Mineral-Rich Liquids': 'Bone broth, sparkling water'
'Electrolytes': 'Himalayan salt, sea salt, potassium-rich meats (beef, pork), magnesium supplements'

Special Section: Living with the Carnivore Diet

'Dining Out: How to Stick to Your Diet in Social Settings'

Eating out while following a **carnivore diet** may seem challenging, but with a little preparation and the right approach, you can stick to your dietary goals while enjoying social gatherings. Here's how to navigate restaurants and social events while staying carnivore-friendly.

1. 'Choose the Right Type of Restaurant'

Some restaurants naturally offer **carnivore-friendly options**, making it easier to stick to your diet. Ideal choices include:

- **'Steakhouses & BBQ Joints'** – Offer grilled steaks, ribs, brisket, and other meat-heavy options.
- **'Seafood Restaurants'** – Opt for grilled fish, shrimp, scallops, or oysters, cooked in butter.
- **'Breakfast Diners'** – Serve eggs, bacon, sausage, and buttered steaks.

Avoid restaurants that primarily serve **carb-heavy dishes**, such as Italian pasta spots or bakeries.

2. 'Customize Your Order with Confidence'

Most restaurants are **flexible** with menu changes. Don't hesitate to make special requests, such as:

- **'Skip the sides'** – Ask for extra meat or eggs instead of fries or salad.
- **'Request extra butter or tallow'** – Many restaurants will gladly provide additional cooking fats.
- **'Order plain meats'** – Ask for steak, grilled chicken, or fish cooked in butter without marinades or sauces.

3. 'Social Gatherings: Eat Before or Plan Ahead'

When attending events where **food options may be limited**, consider these strategies:

- **Eat a hearty meal beforehand** to avoid temptations.
- **Bring your own food** if the event allows it (such as family gatherings or picnics).
- **Stick to protein-based options** – If meat is served, prioritize it and skip non-carnivore foods.

4. 'Handling Social Pressure with Ease'

If friends or family question your choices, keep your responses simple and confident:

- "I feel my best eating this way."
- "I'm focusing on nutrient-dense foods for my health."
- "I love steak, and this is what works for me."

Most people will respect your choices if you keep your response lighthearted and avoid unnecessary debate.

Incorporating the Carnivore Diet into Family Meals Without Alienating Non-Carnivore Family Members

Adopting a **carnivore diet** doesn't mean meal times have to become a battle. With a few simple adjustments, you can enjoy your diet while making sure **your family still gets the variety they enjoy**. The key is **flexibility, meal structure, and a positive approach.**

1. 'Keep Meat as the Main Focus of Family Meals'

Most meals already center around **a protein source**, making it easy to follow a **carnivore diet while preparing family-friendly meals**. Instead of making completely separate dishes, simply **adjust the sides to suit everyone's preferences**.

Example:
- **'Family Meal':** Grilled steak with mashed potatoes and vegetables
- **'Your Plate':** Steak with butter
- **'Their Plate':** Steak with their preferred sides

This way, the meal stays unified, and you **don't have to cook multiple dishes.**

2. 'Offer Customizable Side Dishes'

Rather than forcing everyone to follow a carnivore diet, allow **side options** that your family enjoys.

'**Main Dish (Meat-Based)'** – Steak, roasted chicken, grilled fish, or burgers.
'**Flexible Sides'** – Offer rice, potatoes, or vegetables for those who want them.
'**Your Meal'** – Skip the sides and add **extra butter, tallow, or cheese** for more carnivore-friendly nutrients.
This ensures that **everyone can enjoy their meal** without anyone feeling forced into a specific eating style.

3. 'Create Family-Friendly Carnivore Meals'

Some dishes naturally **align with both carnivore and non-carnivore preferences**, making them **easy to adapt for the entire family.**

'**Burger Night'** – Serve bun-less patties with cheese and bacon for yourself, while family members can add buns and toppings.
'**Taco Night'** – Enjoy seasoned beef or shredded pork with cheese, while the family adds tortillas, salsa, or guacamole.
'**BBQ Night'** – Grill ribs, steak, or brisket while offering optional sides like coleslaw or cornbread.
'**Breakfast for Dinner'** – Serve eggs, bacon, and sausage, letting non-carnivore family members add toast or fruit.

4. 'Respect Others' Food Choices'

It's important to **stick to your dietary goals** without making others feel judged. Avoid pushing your diet onto your family members, and instead:

'**Explain your diet in a positive way'** – "This way of eating makes me feel great!"
'**Respect their preferences'** – Let them enjoy their food without criticism.
'**Encourage curiosity without pressure'** – If they ask, offer to make them a **delicious meat-based meal** to try.
When people **see the benefits of your diet** through **your energy, mood, and health improvements,** they

may naturally become curious about it over time.

5. 'Keep Carnivore-Friendly Snacks on Hand'

If your family enjoys **carb-heavy snacks**, make sure you always have **satiating carnivore-friendly options** so you're not tempted.

- Hard-boiled eggs
- Beef jerky (without sugar or additives)
- Pork rinds
- Cheese slices
- Cold cuts (turkey, ham, roast beef)

By **keeping your own snacks available**, you can still enjoy social snacking moments without compromising your diet.

6. 'Lead by Example, Not Pressure'

Rather than **convincing your family to go carnivore**, simply **focus on your own experience**. When they see you:

- Feeling more energetic
- Enjoying delicious meals
- Staying consistent in your eating habits

They may naturally become interested in **incorporating more meat into their meals**—without feeling pressured.

'Final Thoughts'

- **Make meat the focus of meals** so everyone can eat together
- **Offer flexible sides** for family members who eat differently.
- **Choose carnivore-friendly meals** that everyone can enjoy.
- **Respect food choices** without pushing your diet onto others.
- **Keep your own snacks available** to stay on track.

By following these strategies, you can fully commit to your carnivore lifestyle while keeping family meals inclusive, enjoyable, and stress-free.

Appendices

Frequently Asked Questions about the Carnivore Diet

Q: 'Is the carnivore diet safe for seniors?'
'Yes, the carnivore diet can be safe and beneficial for seniors as it provides **high-quality protein, essential fats, and bioavailable nutrients** that support **muscle retention, bone health, and energy levels.** However, consulting a healthcare provider before making dietary changes is advised.'

Q: 'Will I experience side effects when starting?'
'Some people may experience **keto flu-like symptoms**, such as **fatigue, headaches, and digestive changes**, as the body adapts to using fat for fuel. These symptoms typically resolve within **1-2 weeks.** Staying **hydrated and replenishing electrolytes** helps ease the transition.'

Q: 'Do I need to take supplements on a carnivore diet?'
'If you eat a variety of **meats, organ meats, seafood, and eggs**, you can get most essential nutrients. However, some people benefit from **extra electrolytes (sodium, potassium, magnesium)** or **omega-3 supplements** if seafood intake is low.'

Q: 'How do I stay social while following the carnivore diet?'
'Stick to **meat-based meals** at restaurants, customize your orders, and prioritize **steakhouses, BBQ joints, and seafood restaurants.** When attending events, eat beforehand or focus on **meat-based options available.'**

Q: 'How long does it take to see benefits?'
'Most people experience **improved digestion, stable energy, and reduced inflammation** within the **first few weeks**. More significant benefits, such as **weight regulation, joint pain relief, and mental clarity,** can be seen over **several months.'**

Glossary

- '**Bioavailable Nutrients**' – "Nutrients that are easily absorbed and utilized by the body. Meats and organ meats provide **highly bioavailable** vitamins and minerals."

- '**Bone Broth**' – "A nutrient-dense liquid made by simmering **animal bones and connective tissue**, rich in **collagen, minerals, and amino acids**."

- '**Carnivore Diet**' – "A way of eating that consists exclusively of **animal-based foods**, such as meat, fish, eggs, and animal fats."

- '**Electrolytes**' – "Essential minerals (**sodium, potassium, magnesium**) that **regulate hydration, nerve function, and muscle contractions**."

- '**Fat Adaptation**' – "The process of transitioning the body to use **fat as the primary energy source** instead of carbohydrates."

- '**Intermittent Fasting (IF)**' – "An eating pattern where meals are consumed within a set time window, often paired with a **carnivore diet for metabolic benefits**."

- '**Ketosis**' – "A metabolic state where the body burns fat for fuel, producing **ketones** as an energy source."

- '**Nose-to-Tail Eating**' – "A concept that encourages eating **all parts of the animal**, including **organ meats, bone marrow, and connective tissue**, to maximize nutrition."

- '**Tallow**' – "Rendered beef fat used for **cooking and adding healthy fats** to meals."

- '**Zero-Carb Diet**' – "A stricter version of the carnivore diet that completely eliminates **all plant-based foods**, focusing solely on **animal proteins and fats**."

Tips for Cooking for Digestive Ease and Nutrient Retention

- 'Slow Cook Tough Meats' – "Use a **slow cooker, pressure cooker, or sous vide** to break down **connective tissue** and make meats more tender and digestible."

- 'Incorporate Bone Broth' – "Bone broth supports **gut health, hydration, and digestion**, making it an excellent addition to meals, especially for seniors."

- 'Cook with Healthy Fats' – "Use **butter, tallow, and ghee** for cooking, as they **aid digestion and enhance nutrient absorption**."

- 'Avoid Overcooking Meats' – "Overcooking can reduce nutrient content and make meats tougher to chew. **Medium-rare to medium** is optimal for most cuts."

- 'Use Organ Meats in Small Amounts' – "If new to organ meats, start with **small portions** and mix them into **ground beef or bone broth** to enhance digestibility."

- 'Prioritize Collagen-Rich Cuts' – "**Oxtail, short ribs, and beef shank** are **easier to digest** and support **joint and gut health**."

- 'Stay Hydrated and Maintain' Electrolytes – "Drinking **plenty of water** and consuming **sea salt, bone broth, and magnesium-rich foods** prevents digestive discomfort."

By following these tips, you can **maximize nutrient intake, support digestion, and make the carnivore diet easier to follow long-term**.

1- Video Tutorials Access

Suggested Platforms for Video Tutorials:
- **'YouTube Channels':** 'Look for **carnivore diet-focused chefs** and **senior nutrition cooking guides**.'
- **'Recipe Blogs with Video Content':** 'Many websites provide **step-by-step visual cooking guides**.'
- **'Subscription-Based Learning (if applicable)':** 'Consider **cooking masterclasses** specializing in **senior-friendly high-protein meals**.'

Scan the QR Code to access the Youtube channels.

Click the link to access the youtube channel to learn all about carnivore diet

Scan the QR code to access the blog post

2. Spice and Herb Companion: Enhancing Flavor Without Carbs

While a strict carnivore diet minimizes plant-based seasonings, certain **herbs and spices can enhance flavor** without adding unnecessary carbs or sugars.

Safe Herbs & Spices:
- **'Sea salt'** – Essential for electrolyte balance.
- **'Black pepper'** – Adds mild heat without carbs.
- **'Garlic powder'** – Enhances meat flavor while keeping carb count minimal.
- **'Paprika & smoked paprika'** – Great for adding depth to meats.
- **'Rosemary & thyme'** – Perfect for slow-cooked meats and bone broth.
- **'Turmeric'** – Supports inflammation reduction when paired with fatty meats.

Avoid store-bought spice blends with added **sugars, MSG, or fillers.**

3. Seasonal Meal Variations: Keeping Your Diet Exciting Year-Round

Eating seasonally ensures **variety, freshness, and cost savings** while keeping meals enjoyable.

'Fall & Winter':
- Slow-cooked **oxtail, lamb shank, or beef stew** for warmth and collagen support.
- Bone broth-based soups with **shredded beef or chicken.**

'Spring & Summer':
- Grilled **ribeye, pork chops, and seafood** for lighter meals.
- Air-fried **crispy chicken wings or beef strips** for quick, protein-packed dishes.
- Cold meals like **beef carpaccio or hard-boiled eggs with butter.**

Adjust fat intake based on seasonal needs:
- **'Colder months':** Increase **fattier cuts** for warmth and satiety.
- **'Warmer months':** Lean towards **lighter meats** like **seafood and chicken.**

4. Personalization Tips: Tailoring Meals to Individual Needs

Every senior has **unique preferences and nutritional requirements,** so adapting the **carnivore diet** ensures it remains enjoyable and beneficial.

- **'For easier digestion':** Opt for **slow-cooked meats, bone broth, and collagen-rich cuts.**
- **'For more energy':** Incorporate **fatty meats like pork belly and ribeye.**
- **'For variety':** Rotate between **beef, lamb, chicken, fish, and organ meats.**
- **'For chewing difficulties':** Choose **ground meats, pâtés, and soft-textured slow-cooked dishes.**
- **'For electrolyte balance':** Prioritize **bone broth, sea salt, and magnesium-rich meats like salmon.**

By making **small tweaks to meals based on personal needs,** seniors can **enjoy the carnivore diet in a sustainable and satisfying way.**

Conclusion

Adopting the carnivore diet as a senior is more than just a way of eating—it's a path to enhanced well-being, sustained energy, and improved overall health. By focusing on nutrient-dense, easy-to-digest meals, this cookbook has provided simple, delicious recipes tailored to support joint health, digestion, and vitality in later years. Whether you're easing into the diet or already committed, these meals are designed to make your journey enjoyable and sustainable. Remember, listening to your body and making gradual adjustments will help you thrive. As you continue this lifestyle, may every meal bring you closer to better health, renewed strength, and a deeper appreciation for the nourishing power of whole, animal-based foods.

Made in United States
North Haven, CT
29 June 2025

70204569R00046